GORILLAS
Up Close

Christena Nippert-Eng

with John Dominski, Frederick Grier, Jim Hornor,

Eugene Limb, Sally Limb, and Miguel Martinez

Henry Holt and Company
New York

Henry Holt and Company, LLC
Publishers since 1866
175 Fifth Avenue, New York, New York 10010
mackids.com

Library of Congress Cataloging-in-Publication Data
Nippert-Eng, Christena E., author.
Gorillas up close / Christena Nippert-Eng, with John Dominski, Frederick Grier, Jim Hornor,
Eugene Limb, Sally Limb, and Miguel Martinez. — First edition.
pages   cm
Audience: Ages 8–12.
Summary: "A beautifully photographed look at the lives of gorillas." — Provided by publisher.
ISBN 978-1-62779-091-8 (hardcover) • ISBN 978-1-62779-092-5 (e-book)
1. Gorilla—Juvenile literature. 2. Gorilla—Pictorial works. I. Title.
QL737.P94N57 2016   599.884—dc23   2015005999

Our books may be purchased in bulk for promotional, educational, or business use. Please
contact your local bookseller or the Macmillan Corporate and Premium Sales Department at
(800) 221-7945 ext. 5442 or by e-mail at MacmillanSpecialMarkets@macmillan.com.

First Edition—2016 / Designed by Elynn Cohen
Printed in China by RR Donnelley Asia Printing Solutions Ltd.,
Dongguan City, Guangdong Province

1 3 5 7 9 10 8 6 4 2

This book is dedicated to

Madie and Jonah Doppelt,

Bella and Lukie Gratzl,

Jock and Joyce Hornor,

Barb Murdoch and Craig Dominski,

Tena, Vic, and Victor C. Nippert,

Gilda Schutt and Ana Lilia Torres,

and the memory of Pat Hart and Andy Henderson.

The gorillas featured in this book were photographed in
their habitats as they went about their daily routines.
We used only natural lighting to get the images.

CONTENTS

INTRODUCTION

Gorillas. What's not to love? They're smart, fun, busy, and hairy—from the incredibly cute to the seriously scary. They're knuckle walkers. Vegetarian, too. Who knew you could become that strong just by eating your veggies?

Scientific evidence shows that about ten million years ago, gorillas and humans had a common ancestor. That ancestor would eventually produce one branch of the family made up of gorillas and another branch of the family made up of chimpanzees, bonobos, and humans. Gorillas are not humans, but we are both great apes. Somewhere deep in our brains, we share some of the same sensibilities.

There are approximately 350 gorillas living in North American zoos.

We both love our families and would do anything for them. We get seriously annoyed with them sometimes, too. We take care of our infants and raise our kids in astonishingly similar ways. Leadership, teamwork, and the quest for status are extremely important to both of us. What we say to one another with our eyes and bodies can be even more important than what we vocalize. We both come in different shapes, sizes, and colors, possessing a remarkable range of personalities. Both humans and gorillas have unique fingerprints, but gorillas also have unique nose prints. We share many of the same illnesses, from

Individual gorillas have unique fingerprints and nose prints.

asthma to heart disease. We get up in the mornings, work and play during the day, and, if we have a choice, go to sleep in a comfy bed at night. We also both love good food—and will travel quite a ways for a special meal.

Today, gorillas who live in zoos can provide unique opportunities for us to discover how much we have in common with them. There are approximately 350 gorillas living in North American zoos that are accredited, or approved, by the Association of Zoos and Aquariums. In this book, you'll read about some of these gorillas and how they spend their days, especially a gorilla named Kwan and his family.

Zoos in the United States first started exhibiting gorillas around 1930. As with other species, people were fascinated by zoo gorillas, but they didn't understand their needs. It is another story for the gorillas living in today's accredited zoos. These institutions now play a vital role in furthering our understanding of and respect for these great apes. Armed with decades of experience and an ever-growing body of fascinating research, accredited zoos in the United States and Canada follow important, agreed-upon welfare standards for the optimal care of their gorillas. These zoos work continually to improve and share their best practices with one another. They are committed to providing the fullest, healthiest life possible for all gorillas. Zoo experts work closely with the staff of gorilla sanctuaries as well as with people trying to save gorillas in the wild, where the future of these great apes looks uncertain at best.

There is still much to learn about gorillas. They are currently at the center of a number of important debates. How intelligent, emotional, and self-aware are they? What does this mean for how we should treat them? How can we best protect gorillas—physically, economically, and legally—including those who live in the wild, in sanctuaries, and in zoos? What should be the role of zoo gorillas in ensuring the future of the species? Anytime we take on the responsibility of caring for another individual, there are going to be significant challenges involved and difficult decisions to be made. When it comes to gorillas, new research, ethical concerns, and threats to their survival in the wild mean that these conversations have never been more important.

What should be the role of zoo gorillas in ensuring the future of the species?

Most of us will not get to spend time with gorillas in the wild or in sanctuaries. At the zoo, however, curious visitors can get to know these great apes up close and learn about gorillas both as a species and as individuals. Each gorilla has a remarkable past and is full of personality, emotion, and surprises. Watching zoo gorillas closely and quietly can help us all begin to realize how much we have in common with these distant cousins of ours.

Let's start by getting to know Kwan. He's an adult male gorilla who lives with his family of six females in the city of Chicago, Illinois, located in the midwestern part of the United States.

KWAN
(KWAHN)

Kwan walks quadrupedally—on all four limbs.

There's no doubt about it: Kwan is one impressive guy. He's a silverback, which is an adult male gorilla. He lives at Lincoln Park Zoo in Chicago. Kwan is the leader of his troop and a dad who takes his job very seriously.

If you want to understand gorillas, you should start with one very important rule: do not mess with a silverback. A silverback is smart and curious and might be as interested in you as you are in him. He can be relaxed, kind, and patient. But the moment he thinks you are being disrespectful or bothering his family, he will do his best to scare you off and send you on your way.

Do NOT mess with a silverback!

KWAN

- BORN: March 2, 1989, at North Carolina Zoo in Asheboro, NC
- OFFSPRING: Amare (with Kowali), Patty (with Bana), Nayembi (with Rollie), Bella (with Bahati)
- PARENTS: Carlos* (father) and Hope* (mother)
- SIBLINGS: None
- HALF SIBLINGS: Kwashi* and Kuja*

*deceased

Slim and trim, Kwan is quite compact when he sits. Notice the size of Kwan's head compared with the rest of his body.

Kwan is an excellent example of a mature silverback. He's lightning fast, unbelievably powerful, and quick to respond. Some silverbacks are more relaxed. They just give misbehaving troop members a warning look or "bark" and the mischief makers stop what they're doing. Kwan will get up and make his family members stop what they're doing before they even notice that *he* noticed what they were doing! Yet this massive, foreboding silverback is very gentle when he plays with his kids, and he likes

Kwan may be seen in the movie Return to Me. ▶

Kwan is very powerful and quick to respond.

solving puzzles on a gorilla-sized computer touch screen. Kwan was also in a movie. When he was ten years old, he was filmed while going about his everyday activities for the movie *Return to Me*. He appeared as the character named Sydney.

Kwan's full name is Kwanza (KWAHN-zuh). It means "first" or "beginning" in Swahili. He was given that name because he was the first gorilla born at North Carolina Zoo. He's grown now, and his desire to get up and go helps him stay remarkably fit. He weighs a whopping 365 pounds and eats sixteen pounds of vegetables and leafy greens with a bit of fruit every day. His favorite foods include tomatoes, red peppers, lettuces, kale, and any kind of fruit. He enjoys snacking on crunchy low-sugar breakfast cereals, too, and can pick up a single Rice Krispie with those giant sausage fingers of his.

Kwan was the first gorilla born at North Carolina Zoo.

◀ *Even when he is relaxed, Kwan never stops watching out for the troop.*

GORILLAS AND HUMANS:
SOME DIFFERENCES

Gorilla and human bodies are very similar. For starters, neither one of us has a tail. (Monkeys have tails; great apes do not.)

We have far more in common than that, though. In fact, if a zoo gorilla needs surgery, veterinarians who specialize in zoo medicine work together with doctors who would perform that kind of surgery on humans. For instance, the surgeon who operated on Michael Jordan and other members of the Chicago Bulls basketball team came once to Lincoln Park Zoo to repair the knee of an aging silverback named Frank.

There are, however, some interesting differences between gorilla and human anatomy.

Like humans, gorillas have opposable thumbs on their hands. Their thumbs work from the opposite direction of the rest of their fingers, so they can grab and hold things. But unlike humans, gorillas also have opposable "thumbs" on their feet—their big toes. Being able to grab and hold on to things with their feet makes tree climbing easier. ▶

Gorillas have a crest called a sagittal ridge on the tops of their heads. It runs from front to back along the middle of the skull and is especially prominent on silverbacks. This ridge supports powerful jaw muscles and massive molars that help crush and grind fibrous, woody plants.

Male gorillas are usually about twice as big as female gorillas. Overall, the average difference in body size between gorilla males and females is much greater than it is between human males and females.

Gorillas' arms are longer and more powerful than their legs. They can walk on two legs, but they usually use both their arms and their legs to walk. They support their weight on the knuckles of their hands and the bottoms of their feet.

Gorillas eat a lot of plants. They can look like they have really big bellies because of all the fiber in their diets. Inside those big bellies are digestive systems that are a little different from ours. In both gorillas and humans, the colon is part of the large intestine. It is responsible for absorbing water and some of the nutrients from the food we've eaten before we get rid of the leftover waste. The colon takes up about 20 percent of a human's digestive tract but about 50 percent of a gorilla's digestive tract. This helps gorillas process all those plants they eat.

Kwan

GORILLA SPECIES
BASICS

Gorillas are a type of primate. This is a group of animals that includes humans, apes, monkeys, lemurs, lorises, and tarsiers. There are four subspecies of gorillas. In the wild, gorillas are found living in a region of Africa along the equator. Two subspecies of gorillas are from the eastern section of this region, and two are from the western part.

The eastern gorillas include the mountain and eastern lowland gorillas. (Eastern lowland gorillas are also known as Grauer's gorillas.) The western gorillas include the Cross River and western lowland gorillas.

Kwan and his family are western lowland gorillas. Their scientific name is *Gorilla gorilla gorilla*. Although western lowland gorillas are critically endangered, there are still more of them in the wild than any other subspecies. Western lowland gorillas are the only gorillas found in zoos anywhere in the world.

EQUATOR

In the wild, western lowland gorillas are found in the countries of Angola, Cameroon, Central African Republic, Republic of the Congo, the Democratic Republic of the Congo, Equatorial Guinea, and Gabon.

GORILLA FAMILY
TROOPS

Little gorillas like Patty ride on their mothers' backs. Silverbacks like Kwan keep an eye on everyone when the troop travels.

Kwan is the leader of a "family" troop. In zoos and in the wild, a western lowland gorilla family troop usually has one silverback, a few adult females (known as a harem), and a bunch of kids. The adult females are all the silverback's mates. The troop also includes the females' young offspring, ranging from infants to teenagers. The current silverback may not be the father of all the offspring in the troop.

Like a troop of performers, scouts, or soldiers, wild gorillas are constantly on the move, stopping at good places to eat and sleep along

Here is mom Rollie when her daughter, Nayembi, was just a few days old. ▶

A silverback lives with a harem of adult females.

Strong bonds between mothers and their newborns help ensure the future of the troop.

When they rest, gorillas make sleeping nests.

the way. If they find a favorite food or an especially good variety of foods growing somewhere, they may stay put for a couple of days.

When they rest, gorillas make sleeping nests. The gorillas shape whatever plants are handy into comfortable places to curl up. They often sleep on the ground for daytime naps but up in the trees at night for safety.

At the time this book was written, there were seven individuals in Kwan's troop: Kwan, his harem of three adult females (Rollie, Bana, and Bahati), and Kwan's three daughters (Patty, Nayembi, and Bella). While Kwan's troop doesn't experience the same threats to their survival as do wild gorillas, their daily activities are similar—and their levels of activity are almost identical. The members of Kwan's family eat, sleep, play, and problem-solve with one another, moving between different parts of their habitat throughout the day. These zoo gorillas make nests for

Kwan watches over his mate, Rollie, and their daughter, ▶
Nayembi. A good silverback is constantly vigilant, staying
close to his kids and their mothers.

A gorilla family is often a blended family.

themselves, too, using cardboard, cloth, and mounds of shaved, thin curls of aspen fiber called wood wool.

In the wild, western lowland gorilla troops are highly dynamic—their membership changes often. Adult females come and go, sometimes bringing kids with them from a previous family. Another silverback may challenge the current leader, taking over the troop or splitting it apart. Gorillas are born and gorillas die. Teenagers eventually leave their childhood troops. These young adults sometimes join up with other single gorillas for a while and then move on again, in order to start their own families.

Someone is always in charge of the little ones. Like Bana watching over half sisters Patty and Nayembi, moms and responsible older kids take turns babysitting. ▼

Teenagers eventually leave their childhood troops.

▲ *As they grow, siblings and half siblings, like Azizi (left) and his younger half sister Susie (right), develop special relationships with one another.*

Zoo gorilla troops can be very dynamic, too. Over the past five years, for instance, Kwan's troop changed quite a bit. During this time, his three little daughters were born. Four adult females joined his troop while a total of four other adult females—and Kwan's grown son—left it.

SILVERBACKS

Silverbacks like Kwan are powerful, fast, and resourceful.

Only male gorillas become silverbacks, and every male gorilla who lives long enough will become a silverback. This generally happens by the age of twelve, when a broad band of the hair on a male gorilla's back turns silver-gray. This literal silver back signals to other gorillas that this is an adult male who is now old enough to have kids.

In a family troop, male and female gorillas have different jobs. As babies grow, families help them learn how to survive, as well as how to fulfill their expected roles. A female will need to learn the many skills

As he matures, a broad band of hair on a male gorilla's back turns silver-gray. ▶

Silverbacks are the decision makers and peacekeepers.

Male and female gorillas have different roles.

involved in being a good mate, mother, and ally. A male will need to learn how to be a good troop leader.

In a family troop, a silverback is always at the top of the social hierarchy. There is a good reason for this. The females and all their children depend on the silverback's leadership for survival. He finds them good food. He protects the troop. He decides where they go and when. He helps set and reinforce the social ranking of everyone in the group. He is the peacekeeper and has the final word in settling any social disagreements within the troop. He must be a teacher on top of all this, too, making sure the kids learn how to survive and thrive.

Because his family lives in a zoo, Kwan doesn't have to find food for them, but every day he must do a good job at all the rest of a silverback's duties. In the process, he has to prove to his family that he is wise and fair. He needs to show good judgment in keeping everyone safe and content. If he can't do this, he will not be able to earn the respect of the rest of the troop and keep everything running smoothly.

For instance, each time a new adult female joins his group, Kwan must show everyone that he is being highly vigilant. He has to let the newcomer know that he is the boss and she cannot do anything without his permission until he believes she can be trusted. This reassures everyone else in the family. However, Kwan also has to convince the new arrival that he would be a good mate for her. He has to be nice to her as well as stern about who is in charge. Each time the family expands, the silverback must keep everyone satisfied and safe.

This is true when a baby is born, too. A good silverback is extremely protective of a new mother and their newborn baby. He will stay close to them and keep the other gorillas in the troop away from them. His job over the coming months is to make sure that everyone is careful around these most vulnerable members of his family.

Kwan, looking every inch the mature, magnificent silverback.

Experience helps a silverback become a good dad. Kwan has a grown son named Amare. Kwan learned a lot while raising him. Kwan is not only older now but also more socially savvy as a result of this previous parenting experience. He is able to be a more relaxed father for his younger kids.

It takes a long time to become a confident silverback. Males start learning how to be the leader of a troop when they are very young. They never really stop learning.

INFANTS AND JUVENILES

Newborn infants are used to seeing the world upside down as they are carried up against their mothers' bellies. Like Nayembi, they can hold on tightly from the time they are born. Notice her strong fingers, arms, chest, and neck, even at this early age.

In North American zoos, the median life expectancy for a male gorilla is 31.1 years. That means that half of the male gorillas do not make it past the age of 31.1. The other half live longer than that. The median life expectancy for a female gorilla is 37.4 years. A number of zoo gorillas—all female—have made it past the age of 55. Wild western gorillas have estimated life spans of 30 to 40 years.

Older kids, like one-year-old Patty, ride on their moms' backs. ▶

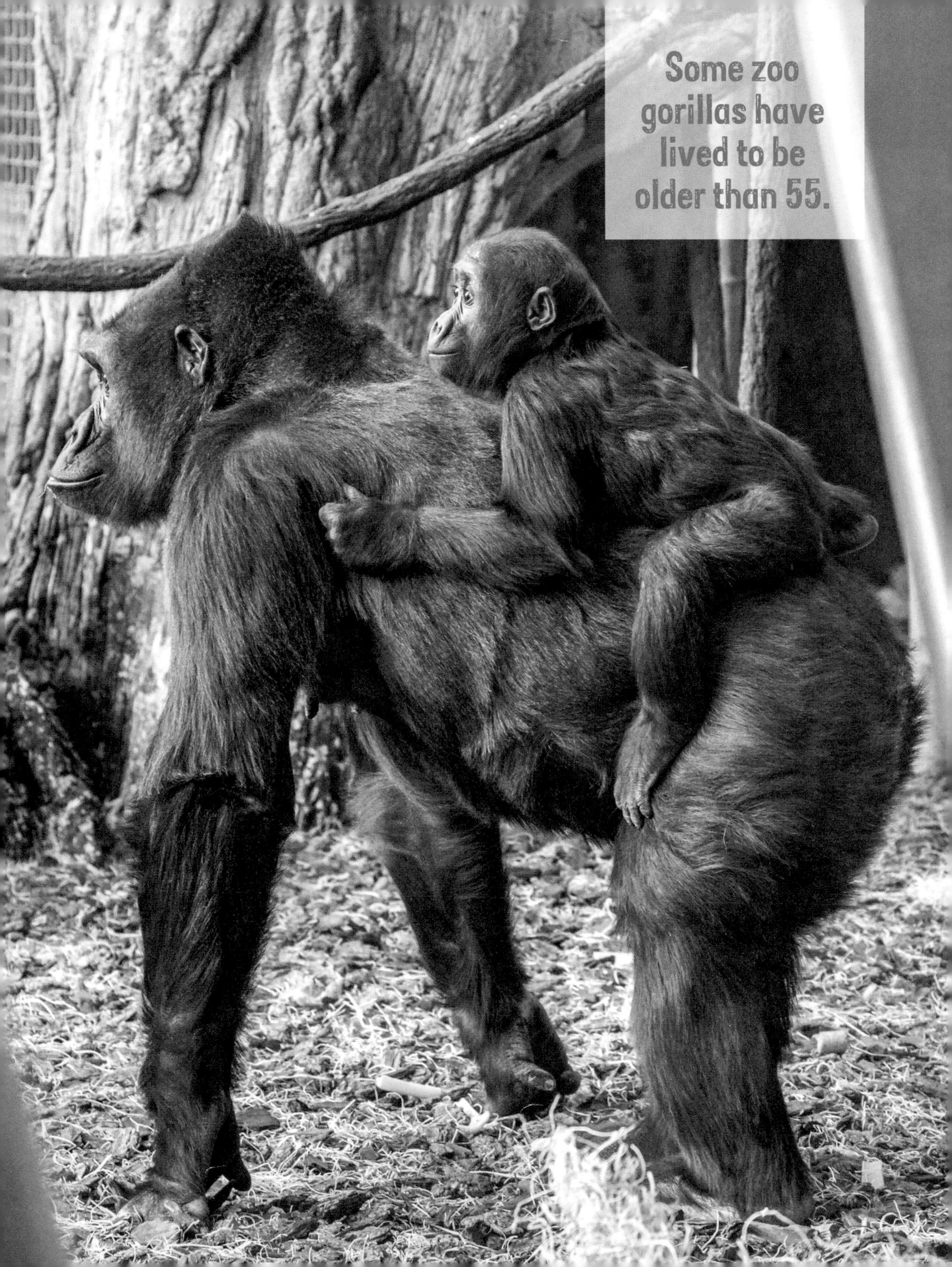

Some zoo gorillas have lived to be older than 55.

Much of a gorilla's development is similar to a human's development, but faster. For instance, gorillas have baby teeth and then they get adult, permanent teeth, just like us. But their teeth come in faster than ours. Gorillas start getting teeth when they are a little over two months old. Humans are usually closer to six months old when that happens.

The emotional part of a gorilla's development is similar to ours, too.

▼ Here is baby Kwan nursing from his mother, Hope.

▲ This is Kwan's father, Carlos.

Gorillas develop like humans, but faster.

It's too cold for her to go out, so twelve-month-old Patty takes in the view through the window.

In general, adult gorillas dote on their babies. Gorilla infants are lavished with attention, although they don't usually start interacting with the silverback until they learn how to walk and climb on their own. Instead, gorilla babies start out being cared for exclusively by their mothers, and sometimes other females who pitch in.

Gorilla infants can hold on to their moms' hair very tightly from the moment they are born. The babies are carried by their mothers up against the mother's stomach until they are at least four months

37

Mothers keep infant gorillas close to protect them from danger.

Kwan's son, Amare, when he was a four-year-old juvenile.

old. After that, babies usually ride along on their moms' backs. They may also wrap themselves around one of their mother's arms or legs. Sometimes babies are so well camouflaged against their mothers, you might only notice them because of a little white tuft of hair on their bottoms. They are born with this distinctive patch. It disappears when they get a few years older.

Mothers keep their infant gorillas close so they can be protected from all sorts of dangers, including other gorillas who might be a little too energetic, careless, or even jealous. But there is another reason gorilla moms keep their babies close. All primates, including humans,

◀ *Here is nine-week-old Patty sitting on Bana's thigh and clinging to her side.*

need the feeling of being held, of being touched. We will not survive without it. In fact, gorilla mothers use lots of touching to teach their kids. Research shows that gorillas gently touch babies and toddlers around the face and especially the jaw and chin much more frequently than they touch older gorillas' faces. Gorillas learn mostly by watching one another. Touching the baby in this area is a way of saying, "Look—I want to show you something."

Gorilla kids continue to be physically and emotionally close with their mothers for years to come. They ride on their moms' backs until they are about two and a half years old and nurse until they're about three years old. Zoo gorillas may drink their mothers' milk longer than this, though. Zoo gorillas don't have to grow up as fast as wild gorillas.

Just around the time they are weaned, the little white tuft of hair on infant gorillas' bottoms disappears. When this happens, a gorilla toddler becomes old enough to be called a juvenile. Juveniles generally have stronger relationships with adult females and other gorilla kids than they have with the silverback. The older the gorilla kids get, though, the more they will engage with the silverback, too.

Kwan lived with his mother, Hope, and father, Carlos, until he was nine years old. Kwan was the only kid in his family of three adult females plus his dad. It was through their example that Kwan began to learn what it meant to be a family—and to be the silverback in charge.

As they grow, gorilla toddlers become great climbers. Notice the white tuft of ▶ hair on Nayembi's bottom. It disappears around the time gorillas are weaned.

Gorillas learn mostly by watching one another.

GORILLA
PLAY

As they wrestle on the rocks, teenage males Mosi (top) and Umande (bottom) demonstrate classic gorilla play faces.

Much of a zoo gorilla's early life is focused on play. Young gorillas love to play—by themselves and with others. In zoos, adults frequently join in the fun: wrestling, chasing, and interacting with objects together. Play is its own reward, but it also helps develop relationships and skills that can be vital in the coming years. When there are no other kids in a troop, adults—including the silverback—seem to make up for it. In the wild, adult gorillas do not play as much as they do in zoos, perhaps

Young gorillas like Patty and Nayembi spend a great deal of time playing with one another. ▶

Play helps develop relationships and skills.

Gorillas laugh, especially when they are being tickled.

Nayembi loves to play by hanging, twirling, and wrapping herself every which way in a sheet.

because they are so busy finding their next meal and looking out for predators.

How can you tell if gorillas are playing? Young gorillas have an open, loose mouth and show their teeth when they play. Sometimes you can see them drawing themselves up to look big, like they're taking a deep breath, then launching themselves onto another object—or a playmate. Clapping, drumming on surfaces, and smacking things all mean "Come on, let's have some fun!"

Young gorillas may also playfully beat their chests. This means they're feeling really full of themselves. It's like saying, "Ha! Look at me! I'm so great!" Gorillas make a cup with their hands when they beat their

A gorilla's laugh sounds like "Heh-heh-heh."

chests. It makes a *pok-pok-pok* sound. Gorillas laugh, too, especially when they're being tickled. Their laugh is a rapid panting sound. It's like breathing in and out very quickly while saying "heh" each time you inhale and exhale, over and over again: *heh-heh-heh-heh-heh*.

If you're not sure whether gorillas are playing or fighting, it's almost certainly play. Fights are not uncommon, though, and when they happen, they're fast and furious. There may be some bite wounds, but individuals are rarely seriously hurt.

When young gorillas beat their chests it's like saying, "Ha! Look at me!"

TEENAGERS

Here is Azizi, not quite a blackback yet but already taking on sentry duties. Note the powerful stance, designed to make him look "large and in charge," as he stands in front of the door to his family's inside habitat. Whenever any of the females went outside but his silverback dad stayed inside, Azizi would immediately get up and go outside, too. Each time, he stayed out—making sure all was well—until everyone came back in.

Kwan was nine years old when he moved to Lincoln Park Zoo. He was a gangly gorilla blackback. *Blackback* is the word for a young male gorilla between the ages of eight and twelve years old. As they mature into fully grown silverbacks, these subadult gorillas will not only develop that distinctive gray hair on their backs and a massive head crest, they also will gain hundreds of pounds and extraordinary strength.

Azizi again, now two years older and a blackback. During the winter, he continues to keep an eye on his family's yard—but from inside. ▶

A blackback
is like a
gorilla
teenager.

Blackbacks help the silverback by looking out for any threats.

Blackbacks act as the silverback's self-appointed assistants. A silverback with a family will avoid dangerous situations whenever possible. Blackbacks help the silverback by looking out for any threats. They act as sentries, helping to patrol the edges of the group. If they see anything troubling, blackbacks will let the silverback know and work with him to help solve the problem. These activities are important for the family as well as for a growing male who must learn how to be the leader of his own troop one day. Males are responsible for this work, although they aren't the only gorillas to do it. Females also help fill sentry roles, especially if their sons are too young or the silverback is the only male in the troop.

In the wild, poachers' traps are a constant source of injury and death for gorillas. Photographs and eyewitness accounts from the Karisoke Research Center in Rwanda tell an amazing story of young mountain gorillas working together with their silverback to protect the troop from this danger. A park ranger had been looking for and dismantling poachers' traps. He knew a troop of gorillas was nearby. The ranger had just seen another trap and was going to take care of it when the silverback gave a warning grunt and the ranger stopped where he was. Two four-year-old gorillas (one male and one female) appeared and raced to the trap the ranger had just seen. They carefully, swiftly dismantled it. A blackback then arrived to join the juveniles. The three young gorillas then headed for another trap, one that the ranger had not noticed, and dismantled that one, too. Rangers had seen silverbacks doing this before, but this was the first time they witnessed younger gorillas doing so. They seemed to have learned how to handle the traps by watching their dad.

◀ *Young males learn protective behaviors by watching and imitating the silverback. This is Kwan and his son, Amare.*

YOUNG ADULTS AND
BACHELOR TROOPS

As he transforms into a silverback, bachelor Azizi is becoming more serious. His younger, more playful self still shows through, though. Here he is, wearing the heavy bucket he used to sit and play in.

In the wild, both male and female gorillas leave their birth families when they get old enough and feel that it's time to strike out on their own. The process of leaving the family can be a long one, taking up to three years. Teenagers might start the separation process by living on the fringe of the troop's territory. They might disappear for a night or two and come back. They may eventually leave for much longer periods but still reappear and rejoin the group each time. Finally, they simply don't return.

Azizi as a young blackback. ▶

Gorillas leave their birth families when they get old enough.

For males, this process starts when they are somewhere between eight and ten years old. At this age, they start to have friction with the silverback. These young blackbacks are getting stronger. They're more independent. They want the privileges of a silverback even though the silverback rarely wants to share them. These gorilla teenagers will start spending more time on their own and with other gorillas their own age, leading up to the day when they will leave the group for good.

A blackback may be ready to strike out on his own, but he's still not fully mature. He is not yet ready to start his own family. Instead, he is likely to join up with other blackbacks and younger silverbacks who are in the same position: too old to want to live with their birth families but too young to settle down. Together, these single males may form a "bachelor troop."

In the wild, a bachelor troop typically has one older silverback, and he serves as the leader of this loosely connected group. A bachelor troop plays an important transitional role for these goril-
las. One day, they may each leave to start their own family troops by trying to attract females of their own. In the meantime, the bachelors look after one another and continue to learn the leadership and teamwork skills on which their futures depend. Young adult males usually spend about two to five years as members of these same-sex social units.

Single males may form a "bachelor troop."

◀ *Azizi four years later, transforming into a silverback.*

Teenage gorillas start spending more time on their own.

Bachelor troops are not the only groups of this kind. Subadult females who are ready to leave their birth families also may join up with one another and a young adult male or two, with an older silverback in charge. These mixed-sex groups of singles are temporary, too.

Occasionally, there are family troops of western lowland gorillas that have more than one silverback. When this happens, it is almost certainly because one or more of the blackbacks has matured enough to become a silverback but he still hasn't left the family in which he's grown up. In these cases, there is still only one leader of the troop. Scientists refer to this individual as the dominant silverback. Any other, probably much younger, adult males are called subordinate silverbacks. If they don't leave, they may decide to challenge the dominant silverback and try to take over the troop.

This is JoJo, Azizi's dad. As he gets older, Azizi looks more and more like JoJo. ▶

BACHELOR TROOPS
IN ZOOS

Azizi gives a bachelor-sized yawn. Note his inch-long, pointy canine teeth. They will grow to be twice as big by the time he becomes a silverback.

On average, gorillas have equal numbers of male and female babies. A gorilla family troop, however, has only one adult male and multiple adult females. In the wild and in zoos, this means there will always be more adult male gorillas than can be accommodated in family troops. Zoos have eagerly embraced the idea of bachelor troops because, just like in the wild, bachelor troops can help solve the problem of how to take care of the important social needs of all these males.

As bachelors age, everything in their habitat must be able to withstand their increasing ▶ *strength—and relentless curiosity.*

Umande gives the door a good tug, checking its resistance.

There is one important difference between bachelor troops in the wild and those in zoos. In the wild, bachelor troops are temporary groups. But zoos often need their bachelor groups to be more permanent. This raises some difficult challenges. Adult western lowland males usually treat one another as competitors, not friends. Even if they start living together as brotherly blackbacks, a bachelor group of growing males will one day be a group of multiple silverbacks. They will compete for dominance over one another. Accordingly, bachelor troops place some unique demands on zoos.

Powerful teenaged or adult bachelors have special needs in terms of their living space, for instance. They need to be able to get out of one another's hair even more than the members of a family troop do. Habitats require lots of nooks and crannies that break bachelors' lines of sight to one another. Having spaces so bachelors can sleep alone if they want and then come back to the group in the morning also can help them get along better. There should be numerous escape

Some gorillas are very interested in tools.

◀ Some gorillas—like Azizi—are excellent tool users. Here, he uses a long stick to fish out the delicious, sticky food inside the tube. Azizi may have gotten his interest in objects from his mom, Makari, who is an avid tool user. Umande, another bachelor who now lives with Azizi, is also very interested in how things work.

Zoos are studying how to form and care for bachelor troops.

routes between different parts of the habitat, so that gorillas cannot corner one another. In addition, the habitat must be dynamic and able to stand up to the superhuman strength of a couple of silverbacks, especially if they're in a rambunctious mood.

Zoos have not had bachelor troops for very long. St. Louis Zoo began forming the first zoo bachelor group in 1987. It took them until 1991 to find the right combination of individuals for the troop to succeed. Today, many questions about how to form and care for bachelor troops still remain unanswered. How many bachelors should be housed together? How old should they be when they're brought together? Is it better to start with a silverback and several blackbacks or all blackbacks, close in age? Can new individuals be introduced into an existing group? What combination of personalities will do best together?

Zoos in the United States are actively pursuing the answers to these and other questions. As with any troop, a bachelor group's long-term success will depend on the individuals themselves and their personalities. Yet zoos are relying on bachelor groups to help solve a pressing problem. Each baby gorilla—male and female—needs to have a good home with appropriate companionship, for life.

Bachelors like Amari and Mosi provide one another with companionship, protection, and the ▶
chance to keep learning leadership and other crucial survival skills.

What combination of personalities will do well together?

MEET SOME
BACHELORS

Kwan's son, Amare, born at Lincoln Park Zoo, is part of that zoo's first bachelor troop. Formation of this group began in 2012. It includes four teenaged males.

AMARE (Uh-MAHR-ay)
Amare is the second-oldest and second-biggest bachelor in his troop. Both Kwan and Kowali, Amare's mother, were extremely protective of him. Like his dad, Amare was the only kid in the troop for most of his life. He gets along well with everyone in his new troop, though, and may turn out to be the biggest of the four.

AMARE
- **BORN:** July 26, 2005, at Lincoln Park Zoo in Chicago, IL
- **OFFSPRING:** None
- **PARENTS:** Kwan (father) and Kowali (mother)
- **SIBLINGS:** None
- **HALF SIBLINGS:** Patty, Nayembi, Bella, Rollie, Joe*, Mosi* (a different Mosi, not the one from Little Rock, AR, who lives with Amare in this bachelor group), and Mumbali*

* deceased

AZIZI (Uh–ZEE–zee)

Azizi is a no-nonsense young silverback, a worthy successor to his magnificent father, JoJo, and very clever mother, Makari. He is the oldest and biggest member of this bachelor group and was the first to cross the line toward silverback status. Azizi looks like a silverback in this photo, but at age ten and a half, he's too young to qualify. Some zoo keepers speculate that a blackback may experience a surge of growth hormones if the troop loses its silverback. It is possible this happened to Azizi when the bachelor troop was formed.

AZIZI

- BORN: December 4, 2003, at Louisville Zoo in Louisville, KY
- OFFSPRING: None
- PARENTS: JoJo (father) and Makari (mother)
- SIBLINGS: None
- HALF SIBLINGS: Nora, Susie, Jelani, and Zachary

MOSI

- **BORN:** October 10, 2006, at Little Rock Zoo in Little Rock, AR
- **OFFSPRING:** None
- **PARENTS:** Fossey* (father) and Sekani (mother)
- **SIBLINGS:** Adelina
- **HALF SIBLINGS:** None

* deceased

MOSI (MOH-zee)

The youngest member of this bachelor troop, Mosi loves to play and get everyone else to join in the game. He brings a welcome, even-tempered sense of fun to the group. He enjoys covering himself with hay and sheets and walking around as though he's pretending to be a ghost.

UMANDE (Oo-MAHN-day)

Umande likes to figure out how objects work and carry around giant piles of nesting materials. He is extremely smart, socially and mechanically. Umande is also the smallest in the group, and he is especially close to Amare.

UMANDE

- BORN: February 18, 2006, at Cheyenne Mountain Zoo in Colorado Springs, CO
- OFFSPRING: None
- PARENTS: Rafiki (birth father) and Kwisha (birth mother); Mumbah* (surrogate father) and Lulu* (surrogate mother)
- SIBLINGS: None
- HALF SIBLINGS: Dembe and Tumani

*deceased

ADULT FEMALE
GORILLAS

Bana with her daughter, Patty.

Both male and female gorillas must be good at survival activities, but adult females have some responsibilities that are different from those of the males. Adult females are largely responsible for taking care of babies and toddlers. They keep them close, well fed, and well groomed, teaching them all the basics, such as what is and isn't safe, and how to behave like a polite gorilla and a helpful member of the family. Adult females also have special demands placed on them for establishing and maintaining good working relationships with all the adults in the family.

Adult female gorillas' roles as mothers are especially important,

Rollie with her daughter, Nayembi. ▶

Female gorillas care for babies and toddlers.

Gorilla mothers teach their children how to be polite gorillas.

Rollie nursing Nayembi on their first trip together to the outside part of their habitat.

both for them and for the troop as a whole. In the wild, up to 42 percent of western lowland gorilla babies die in their first year. Research on mountain gorillas, however, shows that the babies of second-time mothers are 50 percent more likely to survive than the babies of first-time mothers. We now know that having one wise, experienced mother in the troop can make a huge difference in a baby's chances of survival.

Good gorilla mothers ensure that the current kids in the troop get the best care possible. They may even step in and help raise another female's baby if she is not very good at mothering. Experienced moms also give the next generation the best chance of being good mothers. Like the young males in the troop, young female gorillas also start learning how to be good parents when they are very young—but they can only do so if there is a good parent around to show them how to do it.

Good mothering skills are so important to the future of the species that it is common for pregnant zoo gorillas to receive a bit of extra training before their babies arrive. Keepers use something like a knotted towel as a baby substitute. They make sure the mom-to-be knows how to hold a baby carefully. And they reward her for coming to them when asked. After the baby is born, this will let them give the baby a quick visual checkup as needed.

Zoo gorillas can often have babies sooner than wild gorillas. This may be partly because zoo gorillas get such good, consistent nutrition and medical care. A female zoo gorilla can usually start having babies when she is between six and eight years old. A male zoo gorilla can usually become a father by the time he's twelve. Yet zoo gorilla experts now recommend that females should be at least eleven years old before they become pregnant, and that male gorillas should be at least 21 before they become fathers. Gorilla caretakers have realized that just because younger zoo gorillas *can* have babies, it doesn't mean they should; they may not be emotionally and socially mature enough to care for an infant. This is one of the reasons why adult female gorillas in Canada and the United States are given human birth control pills until it is a good time for them to have a baby.

Gorillas may be able to have kids before they are mature enough to be good parents.

ROLLIE
(RAH-LEE)

Kwan seemed to have a crush on Rollie from the moment they met.

Rollie is an excellent example of a mature, adult female gorilla. She is Kwan's current favorite mate and the mother of his daughter Nayembi. Rollie is the highest-ranking female in Kwan's troop—at least for now. The number one female in a family is especially important in keeping the troop running smoothly. Rollie spends a great deal of her

ROLLIE

- **BORN:** October 3, 1996, at Lincoln Park Zoo in Chicago, IL
- **OFFSPRING:** Nayembi (with Kwan)
- **PARENTS:** Gino (father) and Kowali (mother); raised by a surrogate mother, Debbie*
- **SIBLINGS:** Mosi* and Mumbali*
- **HALF SIBLINGS:** Bahati, Amare, Tabibu, Matumaini, Hasani, Jelani, Jabari, Makena, Lilly, and Joe*

* deceased

time managing the troop's social dynamics as well as caring for her daughter. Possessing such a high rank means a lot of work, especially if Rollie wants to keep her prestigious spot.

Rollie is an extremely intelligent gorilla. In fact, she was the focus of a *National Geographic* article because of her cognitive skills. Rollie still knows how to have a good time, though. She has always enjoyed playing with the kids in her troop and will still start up a rollicking good game if the mood strikes her.

◀ Here, Rollie is beating her chest and walking bipedally—on two feet—showing off her full size and powerful build.

Rollie is extremely intelligent and the highest-ranked female in Kwan's troop. ▶

Rollie was the focus of a *National Geographic* article because of her cognitive skills.

SURROGATE MOMS
AND SURROGATE TROOPS

Six-year-old Rollie and her adoptive dad, Frank, in 2002, when they temporarily lived at Louisville Zoo in Kentucky.

Rollie's story begins with a tale of two mothers. In some cases, gorillas are not raised by their biological parents. They may be "adopted" and raised by other gorillas instead. Rollie was one such gorilla.

When Rollie was born, she and her mom were healthy for the first few months. Everything seemed normal. By the time Rollie was three months old, however, her mother had developed a bad infection. She could not produce milk because of it, and Rollie could not get enough to eat. Keepers had to separate Rollie and her mother so Rollie could

Adult gorillas sometimes adopt orphaned baby gorillas.

▲ This is Debbie, the foster mom who chose to raise Rollie and her sister, Mumbali, when their birth mother could not do so.

▲ In addition to caring for his eleven biological kids, Frank served as a surrogate dad for nine other little gorillas.

receive proper nutrition and allow her mother to recover from her illness. Zookeepers took over Rollie's care.

Rollie's mother quickly got better and gave birth again a year later to Mumbali, Rollie's little sister. (Their mom must have recovered quickly to have another baby so soon: a gorilla pregnancy lasts 36 to 37 weeks, or about nine months.) Unfortunately, there were medical complications with Mumbali, too. Once again, Rollie's mom had to be separated from her baby, and Mumbali joined sister Rollie under the care of zoo staff.

As kids, Rollie (left) and her little sister, Mumbali (right), were inseparable.

When they were old enough, Rollie and Mumbali were introduced to one of the most famous zoo gorillas, Debbie. No one knows why, but Debbie never had kids of her own. Instead, over the course of her life, she chose to adopt and lovingly raise a total of ten little gorillas who—for various reasons—could not be raised by their biological parents. Rollie and Mumbali were two of Debbie's adopted daughters. Debbie was their surrogate, or foster, mom.

For a while, Debbie, Rollie, and Mumbali lived on their own. Then they were joined by another of Debbie's adopted daughters, Makari, and Makari's new baby boy, Jelani. They all lived together, next door to a family troop led by a silverback named Frank. Frank was a kindly, tolerant leader whose harem of females and all their kids seemed to adore him. Like Debbie, Frank didn't mind taking care of other gorillas' kids. He raised nine adopted gorilla kids in addition to his eleven biological offspring. Soon, keepers opened the door between Debbie's and Frank's habitats, and everyone could move freely between both spaces. Rollie spent much of her childhood in this supersized, blended family. Her two remarkable surrogate parents—and a whole bunch of siblings, half siblings, stepsiblings, and cousins—taught her everything they knew.

Rollie joined Kwan's troop in 2009, at the age of thirteen, becoming part of his harem. At that time, Rollie's biological mother, Kowali, was already living with Kwan as his number one female. For the first time since they were separated so many years earlier, this biological mother and daughter were reunited. We have no way of knowing whether they remembered each other or had any idea of how they were related.

Debbie never gave birth, but she raised ten little gorillas!

THE GORILLA
SURROGATE PROGRAM

Six-year-old Umande in 2012, when he lived with his adoptive parents, Lulu and Mumbah, at Columbus Zoo and Aquarium in Ohio.

Today, Columbus Zoo and Aquarium in Ohio has developed a program so that other infant gorillas have the chance to be adopted by gorilla parents. Whenever gorilla babies must be removed from their troops, these surrogacy experts help the infants' human caregivers learn how to behave like gorilla moms. If a gorilla mother will not raise her own baby, they will also help identify potential candidates so a new gorilla mom, like Debbie, can take over raising the baby as soon as possible.

Not every zoo has a Debbie in its midst, though. Sometimes infant gorillas must go live somewhere else to find their new mother. This is

Lulu raised four biological daughters as well as the two babies she adopted, including Umande.

▲ The gentle silverback Mumbah had one biological daughter—but also raised sixteen other little gorillas.

79

what happened to Umande, who lives in the bachelor group with Kwan's son, Amare. Umande was born at Cheyenne Mountain Zoo in Colorado. Unfortunately, his mother seemed to have no interest in caring for him, and the other females there did not want to do so either. For a while, Umande had to be raised by keepers instead.

Once he was seven months old, Umande's keepers took him to Columbus Zoo and Aquarium so he could be raised in their special surrogate family troop. This adoptive troop was led by a gentle silverback named Mumbah. The troop also included two possible moms for Umande. One of those females was named Lulu. For her, it was love at first sight. She and Umande immediately bonded with each other, and Umande quickly became a treasured part of this family-by-choice.

During her life, Lulu raised two adopted babies along with her four biological daughters. Mumbah helped raise sixteen gorillas in addition to his biological daughter. Today, both Umande and Rollie owe much of their success to the generosity of their adoptive parents.

◀ Umande and Lulu: mother and son by choice, together at last.

ZOO GORILLA
NAMES

Kowali is Rollie's biological mother. She now lives in a family troop at Knoxville Zoo.

Have you noticed that sometimes it's hard to tell zoo gorillas' names apart? There's a good reason for that. Zoos in the United States frequently follow the tradition of giving invented names to gorilla babies that preserve some part of their parents' names. Sometimes the lineage of a zoo gorilla can be traced just by looking at the names of the older gorillas in that zoo. Unfamiliar, invented gorilla names like this can be a little confusing, though, until you get to know everyone.

For instance, Rollie's mother's name is Kowali. It is pronounced "Koh-WAH-lee." You can hear how the last two syllables of her name

(WAH-lee) rhyme with the last two syllables of her daughters' names: RAH-lee and Mum-BAH-lee.

Similarly, one of the other females in Kwan's troop is named Bahati (Buh-HA-tee). Bahati's mother was named Benga (BENG-uh). Take the "Beng" from her name and put it together with the "AH-tee" of Bahati's and you get "Bengati" (Ben-GAH-tee). That is the name of Bahati's son, who is now living in a bachelor troop at Louisville Zoo.

Some zoo gorillas are named in accordance with a donor's wishes. These gorillas may have more familiar names. However, other zoo gorillas in the United States may be given names in languages that are native to the parts of Africa where wild gorillas still live. This also can be confusing, but in a different way. There are multiple gorillas named Mosi and Azizi, for instance. The name Mosi means "first-born" in Swahili. The name Azizi is Swahili for "precious." No wonder Mosi and Azizi are popular names for zoo gorillas!

◀ *This is Bahati in 2015, when her son, Bengati, turned seventeen years old.*

◀ *And here is Bengati. He lives in a bachelor group at Louisville Zoo.*

The name Azizi is Swahili for "precious."

LOOKING OUT
FOR ONE ANOTHER

Mom Babs holds baby Bana while Bana reaches out for big sister Baraka. Gorillas form close social bonds and learn to look out for one another from very early ages.

A baby's survival and a troop's survival depend on the same thing: gorillas looking out for one another. Like human moms, gorilla moms must be constantly attentive to their babies in order for the little ones to survive. Adult female gorillas have to look out for one another, too.

Like her surrogate mother, Debbie, Rollie seems to have taken on the job of managing and looking out for others throughout her life. She took tender care of her little sister Mumbali over the years. Even when

Today, Bana keeps a careful eye out and takes excellent care of her own daughter, Patty. ▶

Gorilla babies need a lot of attention.

they were very young, Rollie was the take-charge, outgoing sister, while Mumbali was the shy, hesistant one. Visitors loved to watch whenever Rollie would tuck an upset Mumbali behind her like a caboose. The two would walk lockstep until Mumbali calmed down, Mumbali's arms wrapped tightly around Rollie from behind.

When she got older, Rollie would look out for other females too. If there was a younger gorilla who needed some attention, Rollie was there to play with her. If there was a smaller gorilla being bullied, Rollie was there to defend her. And when a new female named Bana (BAH-nuh) joined Kwan's troop in 2010, Rollie stepped right up to look after her, too.

Patty (in hammock) is now learning to look out for her younger sister, Nayembi . . .

. . . and baby sister, Bella. ▶

BANA

(BAH-NUH)

Little Bana riding on big sister Baraka's back. They seemed to adore each other.

Bana joined Kwan's troop in 2010, a few months after Rollie. Bana was born at Brookfield Zoo (near Chicago) into a family of amazing females. They included Alpha, her grandmother; Babs, Bana's mother; and her big sister Baraka, who was crazy about Bana. Just like people, though, sometimes gorillas experience a lot of change in a short period of time. By the time she was fourteen years old, Bana's mother, sister, and grandmother had all passed away.

Gorillas can have deep attachments to one another, and they show signs of mourning when family members die. When Bana's mother,

When gorillas die, their families grieve.

BANA

- **BORN:** March 6, 1995, at Brookfield Zoo in Brookfield, IL
- **OFFSPRING:** Patty (with Kwan)
- **PARENTS:** Chicory* (father) and Babs* (mother)
- **SIBLINGS:** None
- **HALF SIBLINGS:** Kwizera, Baraka*, Akanyi*, and Becky*

* deceased

Caring for a newborn is exhausting for gorillas as well as humans! Bana catches a much-needed nap with a wide-awake Patty by her side.

Babs, passed away, keepers allowed the troop to spend time with Babs's body. Bana stroked her mother's body and lay down next to her for quite some time as the rest of the troop also seemed to say good-bye. When babies die, gorilla mothers show signs of especially profound grief. An entire troop is affected by the loss of any one of its members. Rollie and her little sister, Mumbali, both got very sick in 2005. Mumbali did not survive. Rollie recovered, but she showed signs of grief and sadness for some time afterward.

With Bana's closest relatives gone, it was time for her to start a new chapter in her life. She was transferred to Lincoln Park Zoo so she could join Kwan's troop. Keepers did everything they could to ease the transition for Bana. Lincoln Park Zoo staff had already spent several days working alongside the staff of Brookfield Zoo to get to know Bana while she was still living at Brookfield.

After Bana's transfer, Brookfield Zoo keepers traveled to Lincoln

Park Zoo for several days to continue working with her. As Bana started getting used to everything, her new keepers gave her lots of attention and all her favorite foods. To begin with, Bana had to adjust to a very different kind of home. Lincoln Park Zoo habitats encourage climbing and have large outdoor areas. Bana needed time to gain confidence on the vertical pathways and just being outside. On top of that, there was a whole new family to meet.

▲ *An older Patty riding on Bana's back.*

Fortunately, Bana is calm, easygoing, and infinitely patient. She also had Rollie on her side. Rollie knew exactly what to do with a quiet, timid gorilla like Bana who was used to being looked after by an older, bolder sister. Rollie immediately appointed herself as Bana's new best friend and protector. Rollie worked hard to help everyone in the troop get comfortable with one another. She brought Bana special food treats when Bana would not get them for herself. She encouraged Bana to explore. She would sit with Bana throughout the day, just to keep her company. In the process, they forged a fast and deep friendship. Eventually, in the fall of 2012, Bana and Rollie both gave birth to daughters within one month of each other.

PATTY AND NAYEMBI
(PAT-TEE AND NAH-YEHM-BEE)

Gorilla kids love piggy-back rides, too. Slightly older, slightly bigger Patty has a blast anchoring the bottom while Nayembi concentrates on climbing up.

Bana gave birth to Patty in October 2012. Rollie gave birth to Nayembi one month later. Kwan was the perfect, protective dad, and there was a grand celebration around them. Visitors flocked to see the little half sisters and chuckled with sympathy for the bleary-eyed troop and yawning, exhausted moms.

So far, Rollie and Bana have provided a fascinating study in two different approaches to motherhood. Bana has kept Patty close and had a more quiet and cautious approach to mothering. Rollie seems to encourage Nayembi's active independence.

Gorillas vary in their parenting styles.

The two little ones are as close as can be. They are steady playmates for each other. Nayembi is in constant motion. Her early gymnastics and fearlessness high up in the habitat's ceiling were really something to see. In one area, however, Patty seems to have had even more courage than Nayembi. Patty adores Kwan and was the first of the two to play with him. She wriggled around on her back and laughed while Kwan gently put his mouth around almost her entire body, moving his head this way and that, tickling her with his teeth the way a human dad might tickle his baby with his hands. Then Kwan invited Patty to chase him around the habitat. For months, Nayembi seemed content just to watch them—from a good, safe distance! The week Nayembi turned two years old, though, Kwan seemed to think it was time for Nayembi to join in. He gently pulled her to him and started to play with her, too. All three have been enjoying their playtime together ever since.

Kwan tickles his children with his teeth the way a human dad might with his hands.

▲ *Ta-da!*

NAYEMBI

- **BORN:** November 14, 2012, at Lincoln Park Zoo in Chicago, IL
- **OFFSPRING:** None
- **PARENTS:** Kwan (father) and Rollie (mother)
- **SIBLINGS:** None
- **HALF SIBLINGS:** Amare, Patty, and Bella

Nayembi is the smaller, friskier one of these sisters.

PATTY
- **BORN:** October 11, 2012, at Lincoln Park Zoo in Chicago, IL
- **OFFSPRING:** None
- **PARENTS:** Kwan (father) and Bana (mother)
- **SIBLINGS:** None
- **HALF SIBLINGS:** Amare, Nayembi, and Bella

Patty looks a lot like Kwan did when he was a baby.

MAKING GORILLA
HISTORY

Spoiler alert! This story has a happy ending. After spending months apart from each other, here are daughter Nayembi and mother Rollie enjoying a sunny day together.

On any given day, you might see Patty and Nayembi rolling, jumping, and flipping on the vines while their mothers and father watch them. You might not have any idea that you're looking at a piece of zoo gorilla history.

Just like Rollie had to be separated from her mother, Kowali, when she was three months old, Nayembi and Rollie had to be separated from each other when Nayembi was three months old. There were serious medical reasons for doing so this time, too. Nayembi is living proof, however, that separation from a mother at an early age no longer necessarily means that a baby gorilla will have to grow up apart from her.

Nayembi had to be separated from Rollie when she was three months old.

Sometimes gorilla babies get hurt. In the wild, a seriously injured baby is unlikely to survive. In a zoo, swift medical attention means a greater chance of survival. But if a hurt baby is separated from her troop for as little as two days, she may not be accepted back. What can a zoo do to let a baby gorilla recover from something serious and still not ruin her chances of being able to live with her family again afterward?

When Rollie was little, zoos hadn't yet realized that it might be possible to reunite a biological mother and daughter after an extended, medically necessary separation. With Rollie's daughter, Nayembi, though, it's been quite a different story. Along with a remarkable team of human caregivers, Kwan's family has shown the world that an injured baby can recover and return to normal life with her own gorilla family after months of being separated from them.

Nayembi was rushed to the zoo hospital with a life-threatening injury.

In February 2013, three-month-old Nayembi sustained a life-threatening facial injury. No one saw what happened, but keepers heard Nayembi scream and immediately responded. Nayembi was rushed to the zoo hospital. The zoo team knew that if she survived, it would take Nayembi a long time to recover. They also knew that they would do everything they could to make a reunion with her family possible.

Following hours of delicate surgery to repair the damage, Nayembi stayed at the zoo hospital for three weeks. As soon as she was medically stable, she was taken back to a safe part of her family's habitat. There, the other gorillas could not touch Nayembi. This was necessary

Nayembi was in the zoo hospital for three weeks.

◀ *Holding a toy gorilla, LPZ Curator of Primates Maureen Leahy demonstrates how human surrogates cared for Nayembi while she recovered from her injuries. Here, Ms. Leahy shows how they introduced Nayembi to things she would normally find in her habitat and showed her what a gorilla should do with them, just as Nayembi's mother would have done. These are willow branches. Gorillas like to strip the branches, eating the leaves and then the bark.*

because her injuries needed time to heal. But Rollie, Kwan, and the rest of the family could easily see, hear, and smell her. Then, for five long months, 24 hours a day, trained keepers took turns following guidelines established by the Columbus Zoo and Aquarium and playing the role of gorilla mom for Nayembi—just as bachelor Umande's keepers did for him.

Nayembi's caregivers wore black fur vests, sleeves, and black latex gloves to simulate a gorilla's hair and skin color. They sat with, gently groomed, and slept with Nayembi, communicating vocally and physically with her just as a mother gorilla would have done. As she got older, the keepers taught Nayembi what was safe and what was dangerous just as Rollie would have done, too. By the time she was fully recovered, Nayembi traveled in her human surrogates' arms as well as on their backs, clutching the fake fur on their vests. When the rest of the gorillas were safely in another area, this is how Nayembi's human caregivers helped her explore every part of her family's habitat. They wanted her to be comfortable in her family's world so she was fully prepared to rejoin them.

In the meantime, keepers noted that Rollie and Kwan kept a constant, watchful eye on their daughter. As the days went by, keepers also got busy training Rollie in a few things. For instance, Nayembi now drank formula instead of her mother's milk. Rollie would have to allow Nayembi to continue doing so once she rejoined the troop. A mother gorilla always has first pick of anything her child eats, and Nayembi's formula might have tasted as good to Rollie as it did to her baby. Two keepers worked side by side to get Rollie to ignore the nutritious food meant for Nayembi. One keeper took care of the formula. Another keeper stood nearby, and while Nayembi had her formula, Rollie was given her daily allowance of delicious, small fruit pieces. Keepers continued to follow this system after Nayembi was reunited with her family.

All the careful planning and hard work paid off. Five months after being taken to the hospital, Nayembi was reintroduced to Rollie, Bana, and Patty. Rollie would be the key to everything. Would she take Nayembi back? Would she accept the role of being a full-time mother again to a needy little gorilla who was still not even one year old? Bana and Patty served as perfect role models while Rollie and Nayembi began to rediscover their relationship with each other. Soon, it was as if they had never been separated. The next month, the mothers and daughters were reintroduced to Kwan and the rest of the troop. It seemed to be exactly what he had been waiting for—and zoo gorilla history was made.

Would Rollie take Nayembi back after being separated for five months?

BAHATI

(BUH-HA-TEE)

Bahati with her daughter, Susie. Susie is now grown and lives at Columbus Zoo and Aquarium.

There is one more adult female in Kwan's troop. Her name is Bahati. Bahati is the oldest gorilla in Kwan's harem, and she is as tough, powerful, and physical as a female gorilla can be. She always seems ready to use her strength and attitude to make a point. Visitors may sometimes see Bahati rushing around to gather up the biggest possible pile of biscuits and other treats. She carries them in her mouth as well as her arms. Her mother and her grandmother did the same thing.

Bahati is the mother of two grown gorillas who now live in different zoos. She is not particularly interested in playing with kids, but when Patty and Nayembi were very young, visitors could often see Bahati sitting quietly nearby and watching out for them. They love to be near her

BAHATI

BORN: September 20, 1990, at
Lincoln Park Zoo in Chicago, IL
• OFFSPRING: Bella (with Kwan), Susie
(with JoJo), and Bengati (with Frank)
• PARENTS: Gino (father) and Benga (mother)
• SIBLINGS: Hasani and Makena
• HALF SIBLINGS: Rollie, Tabibu,
Bulera, Jelani, Kivu, Bebac, Matumaini,
Jabari, Lilly, Babec*, Mosi*,
and Mumbali*

* deceased

and have definitely won her over. Bahati and Kwan, on the other hand, are actually quite playful with each other. In fact, Bahati is the one adult female who seems to enjoy roughhousing with Kwan.

When Bahati joined Kwan's troop in 2012, her grown daughter, Susie, came with her—just as they might have done in the wild. Susie was old enough at the time to also become part of Kwan's harem. Bahati had a real challenge looking out for Susie in their new troop while also showing respect to Kwan. Eventually, Susie moved to Columbus Zoo and Aquarium while Bahati stayed with Kwan.

For the next three years, Bahati lived without a child in the troop, until in the spring of 2015, Bahati gave birth to a daughter, Bella. Now Kwan is the father of three little girls, and the troop has six females.

◀ It's a girl! Bahati's newest daughter, Bella.

HIERARCHY
AMONG FEMALES

Here is Bana and newly born Patty. The silverback makes sure that new mothers receive an immediate bump in status.

Social status among gorillas is constantly being negotiated, and it's negotiated with every member of the troop. Any female's status is largely determined by the silverback, who is at the top of the troop hierarchy. The more the silverback likes an individual, the more status that individual will have. He'll insist on it.

Kwan, for instance, seemed to have had a crush on Rollie pretty much from the moment they met. That has certainly helped her reach the top of the troop's ladder. She has also been with Kwan longer

With the arrival of Bella, Bahati joined the other two adult females in receiving more of Kwan's respect. It remains to be seen whether she or Bana will outrank Rollie one day. ▶

Females become top ranking for multiple reasons.

than the other females, and it's common for the female who has been with the silverback longest to have the highest status in the troop.

Some of Rollie's other attributes may also contribute to her rank. Even if a female hasn't been with the silverback the longest or had his baby, she can still help herself rise through the ranks. She can display loyalty to the silverback, earn the respect and friendship of the other females, and use valuable skills on the entire troop's behalf. Rollie has done all of these things.

In general, some gorillas seem to care more about status than others. When it comes to high rank, for instance, there are few gorillas who seem to want it more than Bahati—or less than Bana. Bana is shy and tends to avoid conflict with any gorilla. She is more accepting of whatever status the others will give her. Bahati, on the other hand, actively tries to get Kwan's attention and ingratiate herself with him. For now, however, Kwan remains most interested in Rollie first, then Bana.

Bahati regularly challenges Rollie's status. She does this in one small but highly visible way. In the wild or in zoos, the surest way to figure out who has higher status in a gorilla troop is to watch for who gets out of whose way. This is called displacement. A gorilla with lower status has to displace for (or get out of the way of) a moving gorilla with higher status. If a lower-ranking gorilla is seated in a place that the higher-status gorilla wants, the lower-ranking gorilla has to get up and move before

In general, any female can increase her status by being:

- the mother of the current silverback's child
- the mother of a son rather than a daughter
- the one who stays with the silverback if other females leave

Kwan on the ground with Bana and baby ▶
Patty higher up, sitting on a tree trunk.

the higher-status gorilla even gets there. Gorillas always have to be watching for wherever a higher-ranked troop member is heading. They expect lower-ranked troop members to do the same for them.

It sometimes looks as though Rollie and Bahati are training for an ice hockey game, though. They intentionally bump into each other, trying to be the first to get through the door or around an object. Kwan often jumps up and runs over toward them when this happens, making sure the conflict doesn't get out of hand. He can get quite annoyed with both of them for squabbling like this, but he always insists that Bahati remain the subordinate gorilla, at least for the time being.

- clever at forming friendships and alliances
- good at preventing and solving conflict
- willing and able to help raise others' kids
- a great forager who shares preferred foods with others

▲ *What does a silverback look like when he's annoyed? In the image above, Kwan has seen something going on inside his habitat that he does not like. Other gorillas in his troop are misbehaving, possibly Rollie and Bahati. Look at Kwan's stiff, straight back, his tightly pursed lips, and how he is drawing himself upright, ready to lunge forward.*

For Kwan, it turns out that new mothers are a special case when it comes to displacement. After Bana and Rollie had their babies, they were visibly tired and were not yet very good at walking on only three limbs while carrying a baby. Kwan let them know repeatedly that they did not have to displace for him when he came near. Each time they would start to get up, he would gently touch them as if to say, "It's okay—stay where you are." He only wanted to sit nearby in order to protect and reassure them.

▲

Kwan lunges! He moves lighting fast, keeping himself tall and showing off his powerful, expanded body while propelling himself onward. He is looking down, for this is not a direct challenge to anyone—yet—and his movements are not intended to result in contact. Rather, it is a show, a display of displeasure designed to get his family's attention and bring them to order.

▲

Kwan is coming to a halt and looking at the gorillas inside. He holds himself upright a bit longer to make sure they are impressed by his size— and his wishes. The performance was probably accompanied by a warning vocalization, too—the gorilla equivalent of "Knock it off!" In a settled troop, it is rare that a silverback needs to do any more than this for his family members to get the message and stop misbehaving.

Status often influences which areas of the habitat zoo gorillas routinely occupy. For instance, Kwan is usually found on the ground level of his habitat. Here, he is closest to the food and in the best position to protect his family. Individuals with the lowest status are generally found highest up in the habitat—farthest away from Kwan and the food scattered on the ground. Nursing mothers and infants are found either on the ground next to Kwan or, if they're resting, halfway up, in the trees.

BALANCING POWER
IN A TROOP

In the bachelor troop, Umande quickly built an alliance among the three smaller gorillas in order to offset Azizi's far greater strength and size.

Without consensus about each other's rank, adult females risk more than annoying the silverback; they risk constant friction with one another. Unclear rank means a disorganized, dysfunctional troop. For females, this can include an undesirable, uneven balance of power with the silverback. It is vital that female gorillas work together in order to keep the silverback's superior physical power in check.

In general, gorillas are quite peaceful. They usually communicate by paying close attention to one another's body language and using gentle touches and short vocalizations. Adult female gorillas, like Rollie, can be

In the family troop, an alliance among the adult females keeps things running smoothly. Bahati ▶
plays a critical role in keeping Kwan's superior physical power in check.

In general,
gorillas are
quite peaceful.

A female gorilla will leave a silverback if she is unhappy.

extremely good at seeing and heading off conflict in the troop before it gets physical. It's one of their most important skills.

When gorillas are displeased with one another, however, they can be very physical in expressing that displeasure. You might think that the other members of Kwan's troop wouldn't have a chance against him if there is a fight. He is twice their size. But in a well-run troop, the females work together to manage the silverback. If necessary, they work together to physically defend one another from him, too.

Under Rollie's leadership, Kwan's females work together in exactly this way. If Kwan gets out of line and unfairly picks on one of them, the females instantly respond. They rally around one another in sisterly protection—even though some have a bit more courage than others. Rollie and Bahati never hesitate to take on Kwan. Bana is more timid and reluctant to do so. She seems to prefer preventing conflict in the first place. It is primarily Rollie's and Bahati's willingness to join forces when Kwan gets physical that keeps the power dynamic in the troop stable and balanced.

Bachelor troops may operate this way as well. Umande, Mosi, and Amare all act together to offset Azizi's far greater size and strength. Interestingly, it is Umande, the smallest of the three, who orchestrated their alliance. He also works hardest to keep that alliance together.

But what if females in the wild band together like this and the silverback still won't change his ways? In that case, they may very well "vote with their feet." When the time is right, an unhappy female will simply leave the troop. She will go look for another silverback she thinks will take better care of her and, sometimes, her young kids. Female gorillas in zoos don't have that option, of course. This makes their cooperation with one another all the more important.

◀ *After Azizi becomes a mature silverback, he may one day leave the bachelor group and need to keep his own harem happy.*

GORILLA
HABITATS

The Regenstein Center for African Apes (RCAA) as seen through Kwan's outdoor habitat.

The design of habitats for zoo gorillas is critical for the gorillas' safety and quality of life. In 2002, Kwan, Rollie, and the other great apes of Lincoln Park Zoo were temporarily moved to other zoos so that work could begin on their current habitats in the Regenstein Center for African Apes (RCAA). With 29,000 square feet of living space, the RCAA provides these urban gorillas with homes that are as functionally equivalent as possible to those of their wild counterparts.

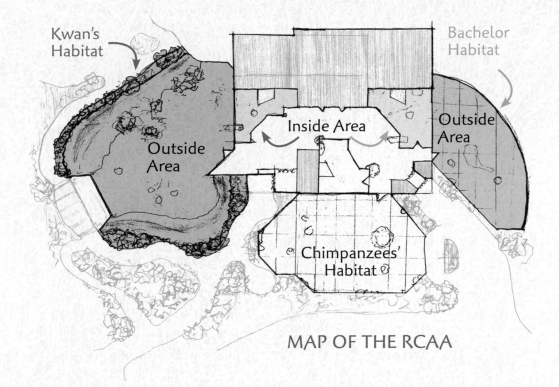

Kwan's Habitat

Bachelor Habitat

Inside Area

Outside Area

Outside Area

Chimpanzees' Habitat

MAP OF THE RCAA

There are three visible habitats here, two housing gorillas and one with chimpanzees.

In the RCAA, each troop has three areas to call its own. The family and the bachelor groups do not share any spaces. Adult male gorillas do not want other males to come near their troops. Instead, each Lincoln Park Zoo troop has its own outside yard and an inside "day room" that are on exhibit to visitors. Each troop also has a third area, located out of the public's view and underneath the day room. By moving the gorillas down here, keepers can clean the areas that are on view, take care of the gorillas' medical needs, and conduct training sessions in a quieter space.

Well-Designed Habitats

Clean and Safe ▶

The habitats must be easy to maintain. Keeping the spaces clean and safe for the gorillas is a high priority.

◀ Functional and Interesting

The gorilla habitats have to be functional as well as interesting for everyone, from the largest, wisest silverback to a wobbly, inexperienced toddler. Every feature needs to support and sustain the gorillas' daily lives.

◀ Easy and Natural

It must be easy for keepers to distribute food, water, treats, and other resources. The gorillas should be able to imitate the ways they would access these things in the wild.

Secure ▶

The habitat must also ensure the security of healthy, hard-playing, even rambunctious gorillas— and any people who are nearby.

◀ Interactive

The habitats must allow the gorillas to interact in many different ways with keepers, researchers, medical staff, educators, and visitors, every day. Both the gorillas and the people need to be able to see what's happening on either side of the glass and feel good about what they see.

KWAN'S
OUTDOOR AREA

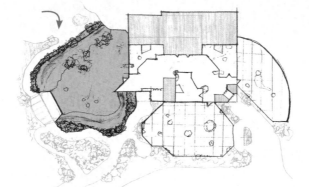

Visitors to the RCAA may get their first sight of the gorillas in the outside area of Kwan's habitat. Three conditions must be met before Lincoln Park Zoo gorillas can go outside. First, there can be no humans in the yard. Gorillas and keepers are not allowed to come in full contact

A **THE MOAT AND HIGH WALL** mark the gorillas' territory and keep them inside their designated space.

B **THE GLASS VIEWING STATION**, with bench seating, is an excellent observation post.

C **STEEL KEEPERS' DOOR** gives keepers access to the outside area of the habitat, as long as the gorillas are inside.

D **OUTSIDE "SHIFT DOOR"** gives gorillas direct access between the downstairs area of their habitat and the outside yard.

E **VIEWING RAILINGS** provide vantage points from which visitors can watch the gorillas when they're outside.

▲ *Kwan outside, snacking on freshly picked grass.*

with one another except in unusual circumstances, as when caring for an infant gorilla or performing surgery on a sedated adult. Second, the temperature must be at least 45ºF (7.2ºC) or higher—or, if there are kids in the troop, 50ºF (10ºC) or higher. Experience has shown that gorillas get chilled easily and might become sick otherwise. Even at these outside temperatures, the gorillas always have access to their day room, where temperatures are at least 70-75ºF (21.1-23.9ºC) at all times. Third, in a family troop, each member takes cues from the silverback. If he doesn't want them to go out, they are expected to abide by his wishes.

Outside, the gorillas have an opportunity to practice important skills. Protecting, playing, finding and collecting food, interacting with visitors—these are all fundamental activities for a healthy zoo gorilla.

They all happen a little differently outside than inside, adding variety to the gorillas' days.

Like their wild cousins, zoo gorillas seem to enjoy the fresh air and changes in the weather. Kwan's females especially love to harvest their own food from the yard. Every plant growing within their reach must be safe for them to eat. Kwan is more of an inside guy, so the rest of his family doesn't stay out long either. However, the frequency of their trips makes it clear that these outside areas have special, constant appeal for them. Like all Chicagoans, after a long, cold winter, the gorillas seem excited when spring comes and they can go back outside again.

The gorillas can be given access to one, two, or all three areas, in any combination. In good weather, the troop usually has access to two of the three spaces at any given time. Keepers use all three spaces in each habitat to manage the gorillas in ways that are respectful and safe for everyone. To shift the gorillas between the different areas, keepers open the square "shift door" to one part of the habitat while keeping the other doors closed. The gorillas see the keeper standing by the door, and the keeper says either "Doors opening" or, if the gorillas have just moved through, "Doors closing," to let the gorillas know what's about to happen. When it's time to close the large glass sliding doors to the outside yard, the keepers ring a cowbell and the gorillas know it's time to come in.

▲

This informational corner next to Kwan's habitat contains the popular life-sized bronze busts of all the great apes: orangutans, humans, bonobos, chimpanzees, and gorillas.

KWAN'S
INDOOR AREA

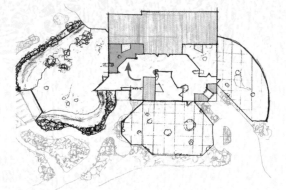

The design of good living spaces for gorillas depends on both art and science. Nearly everything in zoo habitats is made by humans, even though it looks natural. Before designing the current habitats, Lincoln Park Zoo staff studied the gorillas' uses of space and visited gorilla habitats in more than twenty other zoos across the country to learn about the best habitat designs. They wanted the new enclosures to be great homes from both the gorilla *and* the human points of view.

For instance, the habitat walls separating the gorillas and the people are not long and straight; they zigzag, creating multiple corners along the glass. In their research before the design of these spaces, staff members found that gorillas prefer to sit in corners rather than along flat, open stretches of wall. The glass walls were designed accordingly.

A **LOTS OF GLASS** allows natural lighting to flood the habitats.

B **FIXTURES** such as steel "bamboo," strapping, nets, rubberized "vines," and hammocks allow gorillas to make the most of the vertical space.

C **WATER SPIGOTS** are sometimes hard for visitors to see. There are two on the back wall in each habitat so gorillas can get a drink whenever they feel like it.

D LOTS OF NOOKS AND CRANNIES help gorillas find some private time.
E In the family habitat, nursing mothers and their offspring are usually found in
   HAMMOCKS at midlevel.

THE BACHELORS'
INDOOR AREA

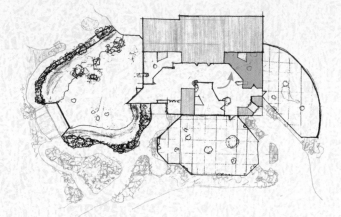

It is easy to see the habitat features and how the gorillas use them in the indoor areas of these environments. Gorillas and visitors are separated only by a triple layer of safety glass. Both groups of primates—humans and gorillas—stand and sit at the same level, shoulder to shoulder, side by side.

Many different experts need to work together to imagine and then create a space like this. Good living space doesn't always stay the same, either. It must change with the needs of those who live in it. In the bachelor troop, Umande has made a special challenge for keepers because he is constantly trying to figure out how all the fasteners, doors, and latches work. In the family troop, everything must be safe for the kids, who are extremely curious and still learning their physical limitations.

Inset photo, opposite: People and gorillas can climb into the popular log feature, each from a different side. The glass separating them inside lets both kinds of primates safely visit with each other in a cozy, fun, and unique way.

A

B

C

Log Feature

A **A WOOD-CHIP FLOOR COVERING** conserves water, absorbs smells and sounds, and allows for selective cleanup. It's easier on the gorillas' joints than concrete. Zoos refer to this as a "bio floor." The wood chips are three feet deep, and the floor functions much like a natural composting system. Keepers use a pitchfork to turn over the top layers to aerate the system every two weeks. If it gets too dry and dusty, the keepers water it to maintain natural, moist balance. Lincoln Park Zoo was the first U.S. zoo to incorporate bio floors into a gorilla habitat design.

B **KEEPER AREAS** are separate areas from which keepers observe, train, and pass food to the gorillas through the fencing.

C When the building opens to visitors each morning, the gorillas enter the day room from downstairs through the square **SHIFT DOORS.**

THE BACHELORS'
OUTDOOR AREA

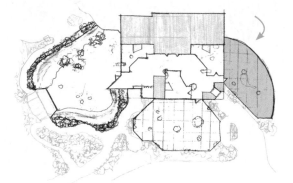

The Lincoln Park Zoo bachelor troop's outdoor space is constructed differently from the area occupied by Kwan's troop. Kwan's habitat was designed for gorillas only. The family troop's outside yard is open to the sky with no fencing. There is only a moat and a wall. Fencing is not necessary to keep gorillas contained.

A TWO DOORS allow the gorillas to move between the inside and outside of the habitat. Typically, both doors are open at the same time. This provides a runaround, so no one gets cornered. Also, if a dominant gorilla is sitting in one door opening, subordinate individuals can use the other door to get in or out. No one is prevented from entering or exiting. The doors can be opened just a few inches to keep the gorillas in but still allow for a bit of fresh air. There are heaters inside along the tops of the doors to help keep the inside warm.

B THE I-BEAM AND STEEL FENCE AND ROOF are sturdy enough even for a climbing silverback. Anything vertical is fair game for gorillas. The bachelors are strong climbers, especially Mosi. You may see them scale the fence to get to the tasty leaves on the tops of the trees—or just to get a better view of the city.

C A SMALL, RUNNING STREAM is good for a bit of splashing fun or to soften up gorilla biscuits, making chewing easier. Gorillas are not natural swimmers, so the water is only a couple of inches deep.

D ROCKS, TREES, AND LOGS. The bachelors spend many hours outside chasing, wrestling, climbing, and playing "king of the log."

Inset: The bachelor outdoor area as seen when ▶ exiting the Regenstein Center for African Apes.

The bachelor habitat, however, was designed to house either gorillas or chimpanzees, so it has some different features. Chimpanzees are smart, nimble climbers and motivated hunters. They are also excellent escape artists. For this reason, the bachelors' outside yard is enclosed by tall steel columns, beams, fencing, and a roof.

The bachelor gorillas spend much more time outside than the family troop. They love to climb up high in the trees. They wrestle on the rocks. One of their favorite games, inside or out, is "King of the Log." Outside, their favorite log rolls a little bit, adding a fun twist to the challenge.

Gorilla Introductions

At Lincoln Park Zoo, the outside area plays a critical role whenever a new gorilla is being introduced to an existing troop. In the United States and Canada, anytime a gorilla is transferred to a new zoo, the newcomer is quarantined, separated from all other gorillas for at least one month. This is to prevent any undetected diseases from being transferred between zoos. During this time, an existing troop may be able to hear and smell the newcomer, but they cannot see or touch each other.

During the visual phase of ▶ Bana's introduction, she remained safely inside the habitat while Kwan's family had access to the outside. Here is Amare taking his first look at the newest member of his family.

Once the newcomer has cleared quarantine, other members of the troop stay downstairs while the newcomer is allowed to explore the day room and outside yard. It helps him or her become comfortable in this new home. Keepers work hard throughout both of these phases to provide companionship and encouragement to the newcomer.

The third phase of the introduction is called the visual introduction. Lincoln Park Zoo troop members are given access to the outside yard while the newcomer is inside, in the day room. Separated by the exterior glass wall, the newcomer and the troop each have lots of space to move around, but they can also safely look each other over and begin to get acquainted. During the fourth phase, the gorillas can touch through a protective mesh. Full contact is reserved for the fifth and last part of the process.

Before long, Bana slowly, politely walked over to meet Amare. The glass allowed them both to feel secure as they began to get acquainted. Bana gave this (obviously young) male gorilla all the time he wanted to study her while conveying her friendly, nonthreatening intentions.

▼

Three minutes later, Kwan appeared, sending Amare away. The visual phase of Bana's introduction continued, and all the gorillas remained safe and sound. The excellent design and flexible configurations of this state-of-the-art habitat made it possible.

▼

A DAY IN THE LIFE
OF A ZOO GORILLA

Zoo gorillas don't mind visitors, as long as they're respectful. They can be as curious about us as we are about them.

Zoo gorillas follow a schedule that is set for them by humans. Because of this, the gorillas' activities depend on whatever their keepers have planned for them throughout the day, week, and year. Gorillas appear to like routine, but they seem to like special occasions, too. Kwan's family gets plenty of both.

Kwan's troop sleeps in the indoor area of their habitat. They are up early in the morning and, on most days, they then move downstairs, behind the scenes, for a couple of hours. They eat breakfast and do their most intensive training sessions of the day while they're down

When she was younger, Bahati's daughter Susie loved to be outside. Often, one of the other ▶
family members had to go out and get her when it was time to come in.

Weather permitting, there is plenty of outside playtime.

▲ *In the wild and in zoos, gorillas are great nappers. Here, Rollie and baby Nayembi doze off together.*

there. Meanwhile, keepers inspect and clean the upstairs indoor and outdoor areas, distributing food and enrichment items for the morning.

At 10:00 a.m., when the building opens to the public, the gorillas come back upstairs and enjoy all the fresh food that was put out for them. If the weather permits, they can go outside whenever they want throughout the day. Visitors are an endless source of activity and interest, of course, especially if they understand how to behave politely around gorillas. Some gorillas are fascinated by babies and children in strollers. Some gorillas look for favorite-colored shoes or clothes. Some look for the familiar faces of people who have visited them for many years. Mostly, the gorillas focus on their interactions with one another.

Gorilla kids like Patty and ▶ *Nayembi enjoy gentle interactions with people, especially children who are about the same age.*

After a long, busy morning, Kwan usually lies down for a nap. This means it's also naptime for everyone else.

Next comes daily afternoon training. Visitors can see the gorillas anticipating this activity. While training is going on inside, keepers may scatter fresh food for foraging in the outside yard, injecting new energy into the afternoon.

Careful research has revealed that wild gorillas and Lincoln Park Zoo gorillas have almost exactly the same levels of activity during the day. Researchers counted every step made by gorillas in the wild and every step made by these zoo gorillas. The results were very similar. There was only one significant difference between the wild and zoo gorillas' movements. In the wild, the gorillas spend more time moving horizontally, across the ground. Kwan and his family spend more time going up and down, given the vertical nature of their habitat.

In the summer, the gorillas stay up longer because of the daylight. In the winter, though, it's clear that the gorillas are more than ready to start bedding down for the night by about 4:30 p.m. The calm, blue night-lights in the ceiling go on, and the gorillas start to make their sleeping nests.

SPECIAL DAYS

On November 8, 2014, the zoo celebrated Patty's and Nayembi's second birthdays. There was something for everyone in the family, from papier-mâché "cupcakes" and balls to colorful sheets for decorations.

Holidays and other special days also enrich the gorillas' lives. Halloween is a favorite with the gorillas. They love to break open and eat whole pumpkins and seem to find children's colorful costumes and masks fascinating. Birthday parties for the gorillas are also great fun. A small army of zoo volunteers makes new, interesting objects and puts lots of healthy treats inside party-themed papier-mâché objects.

▲ Halloween is all about treats: candy for the visitors and whole pumpkins for the gorillas.

When Azizi turned seven, ▶ he seemed to know that the large "Lil' Cowboy" throne made of boxes was just for him. It took him about three minutes to yank it apart.

WHAT GORILLAS EAT

Broccoli

Lettuce

Carrots

Radishes

Gorillas do not eat meat—they are vegetarians. In the wild, gorillas occasionally eat insects, but that's it. Zoo gorillas do not eat any food made with any animal products. All their nutrition comes from plants. The only exception to this is for nursing infants, of course; they drink their mothers' milk. Infants in surrogate or zookeeper care get a low-iron version of human infant formula.

In the wild, gorillas eat food that is high in fiber and protein and relatively low in sugar. Kwan's troop eats dozens of pounds of leafy greens and vegetables each day. They regularly get sweet potatoes to eat. But they get only tiny bits of fruit like blueberries, grapes, bananas, oranges, and apples. These higher sugar, lower fiber foods serve as special rewards during training sessions.

Overall, Kwan's family's diet is carefully controlled to

Tomatoes (One of Kwan's favorites!)

Gorilla chow
(Visitors often mistake
this for gorilla poop!)

Popcorn (If you're a Lincoln
Park Zoo gorilla, sometimes
they sprinkle your popcorn with
cinnamon. That's the best!)

replicate what they would eat in the wild. Their vegetables are usually organic, too, grown without the use of chemical pesticides and fertilizers. Zoo gorillas were once given all kinds of foods that their human keepers enjoyed, including meat and dairy products. But scientists proved that when zoo gorillas ate diets as close as possible to those of their wild cousins', they were much healthier.

Many zoos distribute food for their gorillas to find. In addition to leafy greens and vegetables, you might also see gorilla chow. It looks like small cylinder-shaped brown biscuits. It's nutritionally complete and bought from a supplier.

Wood and
cardboard

Other healthy options could be anything from small amounts of raisins and seeds to vegetables like radishes, tomatoes, broccoli, and cauliflower, or low-sugar cereals like Corn Flakes and Cheerios. On special occasions, there might be gorilla favorites like air-popped popcorn.

Don't be surprised to see the gorillas eating branches that they harvested from outside, or cardboard or the occasional wood chip either. Gorillas need a lot of fiber. These plant-based items are excellent sources of fiber and serve as food for a gorilla.

Raisins

Cheerios

Corn Flakes

HOW
GORILLAS
EAT

Patty pays close attention to whatever Bana eats—and how she eats it.

Like wild gorillas, zoo gorillas are healthiest when they forage for their food. Poking around and looking for small, hidden bits to eat all day long is a constant, low-key activity for Kwan's family, just as it is for their wild cousins. For zoo gorillas, foraging for their food helps take care of everything from overeating and indigestion to not getting enough exercise. During most of the year, there are lots of plants growing in the outside yard that are safe for them to eat, too. They have to work and harvest these themselves in order to enjoy them.

In addition to their foraging efforts, Kwan's family receives small treats like blueberries, grapes, and apple and orange slices during their

Azizi loves gorilla-sized "Popsicles"—big blocks of sugar-free, flavored ice. ▶

Gorillas have favorite ways to eat their favorite foods.

Early-morning preparations . . .

daily training sessions. This is when a gorilla might get some diluted, no-added-sugar juice from the keepers, too. If necessary, there could be some special vitamins or medicine in it.

Just like individual humans, individual gorillas have favorite foods and favorite ways to eat them. Kwan often arranges the food he's collected, then sits down to enjoy his meal. You'd think he was dining at a nice restaurant when you watch him.

◀ *Kwan*

create lots of activity later...

because gorillas love their food!

Azizi loves giant blocks of frozen, sugar-free punch in the summer. He throws them as hard as he can and eats the chunks. Patty and Nayembi will sit with their faces just inches away from their mothers', watching them eat and waiting for them to share. Whatever their moms are eating seems much better than anything else available.

Rollie ▶

FEEDING
CURIOSITY

Nayembi has her own take on the classic (wood) wool suit.

In the wild, gorillas always have problems to solve. Wild gorillas travel constantly. Each day, they have to find food and shelter. They must fight off unpredictable threats to their safety. This keeps their wits fully engaged and their skills sharp.

Zoo gorillas' lives are different. They have good homes, plenty of food, and no predators to worry about. So how do keepers help the gorillas maintain their curiosity and physical fitness while exercising their problem-solving skills? They enrich the gorillas' lives by giving them special objects, challenges, and exercises. Along with well-designed habitats, "enrichment" objects and activities make life more interesting

Kwan with a puzzle feeder full of peanuts, sunflower seeds, and dried pasta. ▶

In the wild, gorillas always have problems to solve.

Once everyone gets the biscuits out of it, Patty thinks a shallow bucket is a great place to sit.

for zoo gorillas. Indestructible mirrors, balls, food tubes from which they must fish out treats, piles of materials for making nests and inventing games, new gorilla computer puzzles and training exercises—these are all examples of things that make a zoo gorilla's day more stimulating.

Anything can become a focus of exploration, play, or comfort, or even an attempted snack for a gorilla. The moment you give something new to a gorilla, it's hard to know what will

◀ *Hollow balls with small holes are filled with delicious treats like sugar-free Jell-O and frozen, diluted juice. It's up to the gorillas to figure out how to get to the good stuff. Like Rollie, they each have their own techniques.*

happen with it next. It's a challenge for zookeepers to find new objects that are safe and interesting for gorillas, given all the uses they may find for anything appearing in their habitats.

Wood chips are a good ground covering choice for many reasons. Because it's possible to pick up only the handfuls that are dirty, wood chips make it easy and cost-effective to clean up after the gorillas. They help prevent injuries if a gorilla falls and may delay the onset of arthritis. And they save thousands of gallons of water, which zoos used previously to hose down and clean the habitats each week.

It turns out, however, that gorillas prefer to sit on cardboard boxes, bedsheets, burlap bags, and "wood wool" rather than wood chips. Gorillas will make "sit-upons" and nice, cushy nests for themselves out of these materials. A gorilla may also collect and then play with any of these; they are highly prized objects. Gorillas may wrap themselves in a cloth sheet, for instance, putting it around their heads and shoulders like a shawl, wearing it like a cape, playing peekaboo with it, or throwing it over their heads and running around like a ghost. It can be hard to predict what gorillas will do with what they find.

◀ One of the many ways Nayembi has found to have fun with a sheet.

DAILY
TRAINING

Visitors can see a gorilla training demonstration every day at Lincoln Park Zoo.

Daily training is an important part of zoo gorillas' lives. It helps keep things interesting, promotes exercise, and allows the keepers to closely monitor the gorillas' health. At Lincoln Park Zoo, everyone in Kwan's family and the bachelor troop participates each day in a type of training called operant conditioning. During these sessions, the gorillas respond to keepers' requests for them to present various body parts for inspection. The gorillas receive small amounts of favorite healthy foods and diluted fruit juice in exchange for their cooperation.

Before gorillas were taught to do this, it could be difficult for keepers to tell if a gorilla was sick. Animals hide illness well. It helps prevent

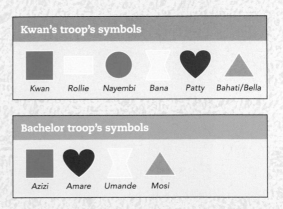
"Open wide, please."

other animals from seeing and taking advantage of a temporary weakness. An individual gorilla could be very sick before any of the keepers knew something was wrong. Now, with the animals' full cooperation, keepers give gorillas a visual, preventive checkup every day. Gorillas are asked to present an ear, for instance, to open their mouths and stick out their tongues, or lift a leg and show the bottom of a foot. Each time, they are rewarded for their cooperation.

Teaching someone to do something by rewarding them whenever they do it correctly is called positive reinforcement. This is the only way gorillas are trained. There is no punishment—ever—for a gorilla who hasn't yet learned a command or who doesn't want to cooperate during a training session. If they don't do what is asked, they simply don't get the extra treat.

Each gorilla at Lincoln Park Zoo has a separate trainer and a special symbol that keepers display in a certain part of the habitat to tell the gorilla where to go for his or her daily training session. Mothers and offspring typically train together. The dominant gorilla's symbol is always displayed first, and his training begins the session. If Kwan doesn't respond to the request to start training by coming over to his place, the group may be given a little break, and then a second attempt is made. If he is still not interested, training is canceled for everyone, because training is

Kwan's troop's symbols

Kwan	Rollie	Nayembi	Bana	Patty	Bahati/Bella

Bachelor troop's symbols

Azizi	Amare	Umande	Mosi

completely voluntary. Kwan almost always volunteers, though, because he seems to enjoy this activity. After a few minutes of working only with him, the keepers will invite the other gorillas to begin their training sessions.

Keepers wear surgical masks and latex gloves when they train the gorillas. Gorillas can get many of the same illnesses that we do. These masks and gloves are worn so the gorillas do not catch any colds or other illnesses from the keepers, and vice versa.

The keeper asks Azizi to ▶ press his chest up against the fence.

◀ Because Azizi did so, he gets an orange slice.

TRAINING FOR RESEARCH
ON HOW
GORILLAS THINK

There is a second type of training in which Kwan, Rollie, and some of the other gorillas participate. This is training that aims to study gorilla cognition; that is, research on how gorillas think. Through this training, gorillas can learn to use a computer touch screen and respond to various images that appear on it. Researchers watch how gorillas respond during these sessions in order to gather information about how gorillas learn. Studies show that gorillas may learn in a way that is similar to ours.

During these sessions, a gorilla is shown a series of colored symbols on a computer screen. The gorilla is asked to identify those symbols in a particular order. This is like asking a human to point to the numbers one through ten—or the letters of the alphabet—in their correct order.

▲ Kwan is shown this layout.

▲ He starts off great, touching the white O.

All gorillas start by identifying a single symbol. For Kwan, it was the white O. His session would start with a screen showing a white O. If he chose to touch the white O, he got a reward. Kwan's favorite reward is a frozen grape.

Once Kwan did this correctly 85 percent of the time, a new symbol was added to the sequence—a red X. Now Kwan had to first touch the white O, then touch the red X in order to get a grape. The first four symbols of Kwan's sequence go like this: the white O, a red X, a green I, then a blue Σ (the Greek letter *sigma*).

If Kwan selects a symbol out of order, then a red screen appears. There is a short pause. The screen resets to how it previously appeared. If he feels like it, Kwan will try again.

Kwan is up to a seven-symbol sequence now. Every time he succeeds in getting them all right, Kwan receives a reward. Then the computer

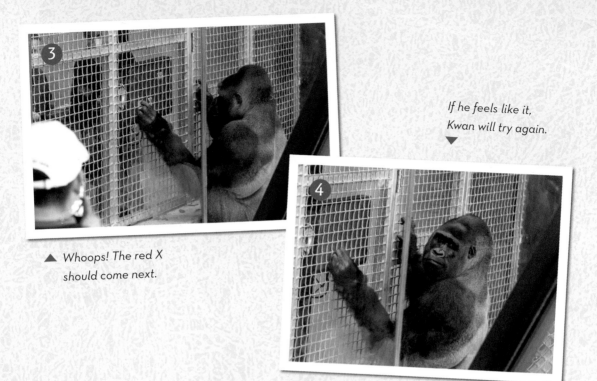

If he feels like it, Kwan will try again.
▼

▲ *Whoops! The red X should come next.*

program jumbles up the symbols again for his next try. The same symbols will appear, but they'll be in different places on the screen. It's up to Kwan to touch them in the right order each time, no matter where they are on the screen.

The gorillas who choose to do the touch-screen activities get special food rewards for their efforts. They seem to enjoy tackling challenging problems of this kind and participating in these interactions. Zoo gorillas are just beginning to help scientists understand and prove how smart these great apes are.

Gorillas are smart and can learn to identify symbols in order.

THE GORILLA SPECIES
SURVIVAL PLAN

Western lowland gorillas are critically endangered in the wild due to people moving into the gorillas' territory and destroying the forest for timber, palm oil plantations, and mining. Wild gorillas are also threatened by the illegal hunting of gorillas in order to eat or sell them, by human warfare (with the gorillas getting caught in the middle), and by the Ebola virus, which can kill gorillas, humans, and other primates. Very few of these gorillas exist in their native African habitat now. As a result, today's zoos do the best they can to ensure the future of this species. U.S. zoos help protect the wild gorillas by supporting and working with researchers and sanctuaries in Africa. Their main job, however, is to carefully manage the population of zoo gorillas.

Former Lincoln Park Zoo Residents

Following Gorilla Species Survival Plan recommendations, here are some of the gorillas who used to live at Lincoln Park Zoo but now live elsewhere.

Tabibu is Rollie ▶ and Bahati's half sister. She moved to Columbus Zoo and Aquarium at just about the same time that Umande was transferred from there to Lincoln Park Zoo.

▲ *JoJo, Azizi's dad, left Lincoln Park Zoo to live at Brookfield Zoo. He had a new baby daughter, Nora, within a year.*

◀ *Susie, Bahati's daughter and Azizi's half sister, moved to Columbus Zoo and Aquarium.*

▲ *Azizi's mom, Makari, was transferred to Kansas City Zoo to help form that zoo's first family troop.*

153

In order to do this, these zoos cooperate in ways that were unheard of even thirty years ago. Today's Species Survival Plans, or SSPs, are excellent examples of this cooperation. The Association of Zoos and Aquariums in the United States has developed more than 450 SSPs to make sure that the future will include healthy zoo populations of hundreds of endangered species.

Each year, a group of dedicated keepers, scientists, veterinarians, and specialists from all over the country consider how to ensure the future of today's zoo gorillas. The result is the Gorilla SSP. Every accredited zoo with gorillas is represented in this process. The group discusses the status of each gorilla, including all the gorillas' genetic histories. They talk about the wants and needs of each zoo. They consider the long-term needs of the overall population. They consider the special needs of each individual. And they try to predict how many homes they will need for all the

gorillas in the coming years, taking into account their sex, age, and, especially in the case of males, ability to live with others. Individual gorillas' best interests are kept in mind first and foremost, but the long-term survival of the species has to be considered, too. Each zoo no longer thinks only about its own gorillas but about what's best for all the gorillas across the country.

The Gorilla SSP regularly meets to review and revise recommendations for changes in the overall U.S. zoo gorilla population. There are recommendations for who should have babies and for the formation of new troops. After special consideration, there also are recommendations for who should be transferred, where they should go, and why. A low-status female who has never had a baby, for instance, might be a priority for a transfer to another zoo, where she could have a chance to become a mother. If a silverback dies, then another silverback who has been living on his own or with a group of bachelors might get a chance to lead his own family troop. The decision to move a highly social being like a gorilla is never taken lightly.

Anytime you visit a zoo, you may find some changes in the gorillas who live there. Some of these changes may have been years in the making. Some of them might be fairly sudden. The people behind the Gorilla Species Survival Plan play a vital role in managing the future of all zoo gorillas.

TIPS FOR
IDENTIFICATION

Every gorilla has a story, whether she or he lives in the wild, a rescue sanctuary, or a zoo. Perhaps you will visit one of these places and find out more about gorillas for yourself. You can start by watching closely.

Keeping track of who's who is a bit tricky at first. We can use gorillas' looks and their unique behaviors to tell them apart. When getting started, we mostly rely on looks.

Size: How big is a gorilla compared with the others in the troop? Kwan and Azizi are the biggest in their troops. The other gorillas may be more similar in size, but still, the size of a particular gorilla compared with others is a good clue for identification.

Hair: Like humans, each gorilla's hair is distinctive in terms of its color, length, and texture. Colorwise, western lowland gorillas have a base color of black, with more or less gray. Individual gorillas may have beautiful red or auburn hair, too, especially around the head. They can have quite distinctive saddles of color across their backs, or random patches of white that are unique. Infants and toddlers always have a white tuft of hair on their bottoms.

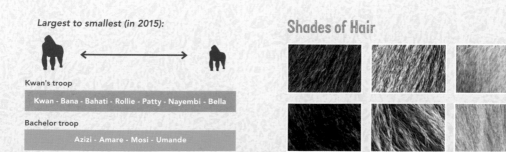

Largest to smallest (in 2015):

Kwan's troop

Kwan - Bana - Bahati - Rollie - Patty - Nayembi - Bella

Bachelor troop

Azizi - Amare - Mosi - Umande

Shades of Hair

Body: Body types are quite useful for telling gorillas apart. Is the gorilla short and chunky or taller and more slender? Look for things like visible breasts, too. If you see them, that gorilla is or likely was a nursing mother at some point.

Head: Gorillas have different head shapes. The profile of a gorilla's head is an especially useful clue for identification. For instance, Kwan has a large head crest, a kind of extra-large bump on the top of his head. Bana has a cone-shaped head. Bahati has a crest like a cardinal on top of her head, and gray muttonchop sideburns—just like her mother, grandmother, and great-grandmother did. Her daughter, Susie, has these features too.

Face: If you study the photos in this book, you will quickly notice how unique each individual's face is. Consider the face shape and the look of the eyes and brow. What is the shape and coloration of the lips? Are there unique patches of color or types of hair around the face?

Nose: A gorilla's nose is like a human's fingerprint. No two are exactly alike. If you want to be totally positive about who you're looking at, go for the nose. This can be really hard to do in person, but use the individual photos in this book and give it a try!

Head Shapes

Kwan

Bana   Bahati

Susie

Noses

Here's a fun test. Whose noses are these?*

A.   B.   C.   D.

157

* Answers: A. Bahati, B. Rollie, C. Azizi, D. Bana

TIPS FOR WATCHING AND
PHOTOGRAPHING

How to Watch Gorillas

If you follow these tips, the gorillas will notice
and probably become interested in you in return.

Be quiet. Some zoo visitors bang on the glass, make noises,
and yell at the gorillas (and one another). In gorilla society,
that behavior is extremely rude. You must be quiet if you
want to learn what gorillas are really like.

Sit, if possible. Gorillas can feel threatened if you tower over
them. Turn your body sideways while observing. Sit or stand
in profile. Looking straight on at a gorilla may be considered
aggressive. Look at how they sit relative to one another
and copy this behavior.

Glance repeatedly. That's how gorillas look at one another—
watch them and you'll see. Staring is not polite gorilla behavior.
Only infant and toddler gorillas are allowed to stare, because
they haven't learned proper gorilla behavior yet.

**If a gorilla makes eye contact with you, quickly look away and
downward for a second.** It's a way of saying, "You caught me.

I'm really interested in you. But only in a respectful way." They'll immediately notice you if you do this. And they might return the favor by repeatedly glancing back at you. If you've really captured their interest, a gorilla might then casually walk past you or even come over to sit by you. You should feel very flattered.

If a gorilla makes you smile, try not to show your teeth. Showing teeth can be a sign of aggression among adult gorillas. Gorillas have a sense of humor. They laugh. But adult gorillas don't show their teeth to indicate happiness.

Stay awhile. Most visitors spend seconds looking at a zoo animal and move on. If you want to understand gorillas, you have to watch them carefully. If you come back every week and spend an hour or so politely visiting with them, you will get to know them. The gorillas will certainly become interested in you, too.

How to Photograph Gorillas

Turn off the flash! The glare off the glass will ruin your picture. The gorillas probably don't like flashes going off at them all day either.

Don't stay in one place for too long. This is especially important if you have a big camera and lens and/or are with a large man. The silverback will be happier if you don't look as if you're standing there staring in at his family and planning something.

Be aware of the light. If you're inside, compose your photo with the outside light off to your side or behind you. Otherwise, the gorillas may be backlit and appear only as dark silhouettes.

WHEN THEY
WERE YOUNGER

Kwan's Troop

Mother Hope with Kwan ▲
at five months.

▲ Rollie with her daughter,
Nayembi, at one month.

Surrogate mother Debbie ▶
with Rollie at about three
years of age.

Bahati at four months.

▲ Mom Babs with Bana at one month.

▼ Mom Bana with Patty at two months.

The Bachelor Troop

Mom Kowali with Amare ▶ at about two months.

◀ Dad Fossey and mom Sekani with Mosi at three months.

Dad JoJo ▶
and Azizi at
two years of age.

◀ Umande at fifteen months.

163

RESOURCES FOR YOUR OWN GORILLA RESEARCH

Researchers often rely on several methods in order to explore the subjects in which they are interested. For this book, we relied on two types of primary, or firsthand, research techniques. We also turned to different sources for our secondary research, in which we learned about gorillas from other people's published research and writings.

For our primary research, we spent hundreds of hours observing zoo gorillas. Our observations were mostly at Lincoln Park Zoo, but we also visited the Bronx Zoo, Brookfield Zoo, Columbus Zoo and Aquarium, Disney's Animal Kingdom, Kansas City Zoo, St. Louis Zoo, and Zoo Atlanta. While watching the gorillas, we took handwritten notes and photographs and also sketched what we saw. Once we felt confident in what we were seeing, we began talking with longtime, knowledgeable visitors as well as keepers, curators, and researchers. We discussed gorilla troops, individual gorillas, and the challenges of caring for them in zoos.

Our secondary research benefited greatly from articles in newspapers, professional newsletters, and scientific journals, as well as online-only content about zoo gorillas. We learned about the history of specific Lincoln Park Zoo gorillas and the nature and needs of gorillas more generally this way, along with a number of documentary films and YouTube clips. We also visited the library and our local bookstores, of course, reading a variety of books on our subject.

If you are interested in doing your own research on gorillas, there are plenty of resources available. Here are some of our favorites:

Websites

Lincoln Park Zoo—lpzoo.org

Lincoln Park Zoo is in the middle of Chicago, free, and open 365 days a year. Check out the website for more information about Lincoln Park Zoo's gorillas, its research program focused on great apes—including gorillas—and special educational events.

Columbus Zoo and Aquarium—columbuszoo.org

Home of Colo, the first zoo-born gorilla in the United States, this place is jam-packed with gorilla history. This zoo is well-known for its gorilla surrogate program and care of individuals with a variety of medical complications. (If you visit, check out the bonobos.)

Jim Davis's Unofficial Gorilla Studbook—dewarwildlife.org/jrdavis-gorilla-studbook/

Jim and Linda Davis are avid gorilla groupies. With the help of other citizen scientists, they are continually updating this valuable resource. Anyone can do genealogical research on zoo gorillas using this tool.

Gorilla Gazette—gorillagazette.com

Started in 1987 by keepers at Columbus Zoo, this newsletter is filled with fascinating insights about caring for zoo gorillas. It was originally intended to be by keepers, for keepers, but it's a great read for any gorilla researcher or enthusiast.

Gorilla Species Survival Plan (SSP)—gorillassp.org

The Gorilla Species Survival Plan is updated every year. This website is loaded with information about how the SSP works, individual gorillas, the people working to save them, and the latest research on zoo gorillas.

Association of Zoos and Aquariums (AZA)—aza.org

The AZA sets the standards for the care of animals living in zoos and aquariums. This organization plays an ever-greater role around the world in supporting conservation and education about gorillas and other animals.

Great Apes Survival Partnership (GRASP)—un-grasp.org

GRASP includes many nations, nongovernmental organizations, and conservation groups. GRASP aids gorillas by helping all primates to live together respectfully, including humans.

Dian Fossey Gorilla Fund International—gorillafund.org

No list of gorilla resources would be complete without the Dian Fossey Gorilla Fund International. Dian Fossey started studying mountain gorillas in 1966. This website provides reports on research, conservation efforts, and the people and gorillas at the center of the organization's daily activities.

Gorilla Doctors Blog—gorilladoctorsblog.org
  Dedicated to mountain gorillas, this website includes incredible stories of rescue, rehabilitation, and cooperation to save the 780 remaining wild mountain gorillas, as well as a few Grauer's (eastern lowland) gorillas.

National Geographic and National Geographic Kids—nationalgeographic.com, kids.nationalgeographic.com
  National Geographic continues to set a standard in helping us understand life of all kinds around the world. You can find fascinating reports, photos, and videos on zoo and wild gorillas as well as other great apes at both of these websites.

The New York Times—nytimes.com
  You would be surprised how many articles *The New York Times* publishes on gorillas, and on the great apes and other primates in general. You can easily search for these articles and even set an automatic e-mail alert to send you a notice every time there is an article that mentions gorillas.

Live Science—livescience.com
  Looking for summaries of the latest research on gorillas in zoos and in the wild? Here, reporters comb professional journals like *Science* and *Nature*. Then they write articles for nonscientists about the researchers' findings.

Zoo Biology—onlinelibrary.wiley.com/journal/10.1002/(ISSN)1098-2361
  The journal *Zoo Biology* publishes the latest science findings on zoo gorillas. It's a peer-reviewed journal—scientists write the articles, and other scientists review them. Find it through a local library, grab a dictionary, and then go for it.

Ethologists for the Ethical Treatment of Animals/Citizens for Responsible Animal Behavior Studies—ethologicalethics.org
  Jane Goodall, famous throughout the world for her research on wild chimpanzees, and Marc Bekoff, an animal behaviorist, started this group in order to promote animal research that respects the animals. It is a great source for information on animal intelligence and emotion, as well as guidelines for conducting research that involves animals.

Movies

Gorillas in the Mist
  Starring Sigourney Weaver, this inspiring film is an award-winning portrayal of mountain gorilla researcher Dian Fossey. The movie tells the story of Fossey's early research years and the challenges she faced as she lived with, studied, and tried to protect her beloved gorillas. Fossey started the Karisoke Research Center in Rwanda, where she

was found murdered in 1985. She is buried there next to her favorite gorilla, Digit, who had been killed by poachers.

The Gorilla King

A Nature documentary, this movie tells the extraordinary story of the great silverback Titus. He was a mountain gorilla whose life was documented since birth, thanks to the work of Dian Fossey and the researchers who continued her work. It is a riveting tale.

The Urban Gorilla

A National Geographic movie by Allison Argo, this feature documents a vital transformation in how we think about and care for zoo gorillas. This movie includes footage of a gorilla named Ivan, showing both his lonely, terribly sad living conditions in a shopping mall as well as the far better home he eventually moved to in Zoo Atlanta, two years after this film was made. Ivan passed away at the very old gorilla age of 50. The wonderful novel *The One and Only Ivan* by Katherine Applegate is based on Ivan's life.

Virunga

Virunga is a documentary by Orlando von Einsiedel about the impact of civil war and the discovery of rare natural resources where wild gorillas live in Africa. These events affect both mountain gorillas and the heroic rangers of Virunga National Park who try to protect them. It is a stunning movie, making it clear that the fate of wild gorillas is interwoven with the fates of all people who want to use the natural resources surrounding them.

Books

Faulconer, Maria. *A Mom for Umande*. New York: Dial Books for Young Readers, 2014.
This is a heartwarming picture book about Umande's adoption and the surrogate parents—both human and gorilla—who raised him.

Fisher, Lester E. *Dr. Fisher's Life on the Ark*. Evanston, IL: Racom Communications, 2005.
For thirty years, Lester Fisher served Lincoln Park Zoo, first as the zoo's veterinarian and then as its director. He oversaw a number of path-breaking changes in how U.S. zoos cared for and thought about gorillas. In this autobiography, he writes about those changes and his life caring for gorillas as well as other animals. The book is dedicated to Bushman, the zoo's first gorilla.

Nichols, Michael, with Elizabeth Carney. *Face to Face with Gorillas*. Washington, DC: National Geographic, 2009.
Michael Nichols is an expert on gorillas as well as an editor and wildlife photographer for *National Geographic*. This is an excellent, easy-to-read introduction to the challenges of protecting wild gorillas—and what it's like to spend your life studying and documenting their lives.

Pimm, Nancy Rose. *Colo's Story: The Life of One Grand Gorilla*. Powell, OH: Columbus Zoo and Aquarium, 2011.

At the time we were writing this book, Colo was not only the first zoo-born gorilla and the oldest gorilla living in captivity, but she had just celebrated her fifty-eighth birthday! This book is a kind of time capsule, showing much of Colo's history as well as the incredible transformation in zoo gorillas' daily lives during these almost sixty years.

Pimm, Nancy Rose. *The Heart of the Beast: Eight Great Gorilla Stories*. Plain City, OH: Darby Creek Publishers, 2007.

Every gorilla has an amazing life story waiting to be discovered, including the zoo gorillas featured in this book. Two of them, Binti Jua and Babs, are closely connected to gorillas you've met here: Azizi's dad, JoJo, is now Binti Jua's mate, and Babs is Bana's mother. Pimm's book is chock-full of fascinating, expert facts about gorillas, too.

Redmond, Ian. *Gorilla, Monkey and Ape*. New York: Dorling Kindersley, 2000.

A good overview of different kinds of primates, this book compares and contrasts gorillas with the other members of this group of mammals, including humans. It's a good place to get started if you want a lot of facts about a lot of different primates.

Rosenthal, Mark, Carole Tauber and Edward Uhlir. *The Ark in the Park: The Story of Lincoln Park Zoo*. Chicago: University of Illinois Press, 2003.

This book has many historical details about the gorillas who have lived at Lincoln Park Zoo, including the changes in their habitat design over the years.

Turner, Pamela S. *Gorilla Doctors: Saving Endangered Great Apes*. Boston: Houghton Mifflin, 2008.

Part of the "Scientists in the Field" series, this is a picture book for older readers on the efforts to save wild gorillas from poachers and other threats to their survival. From the challenges of providing medical care and researching in the field to the challenges of saving orphans and working together with local residents to educate the next generation, this is an excellent overview of the issues involved in trying to protect wild gorillas and some of the people dedicating their lives to this cause.

ACKNOWLEDGMENTS

We owe a debt of thanks to many people without whose support and effort this book could not have been realized: Dominic Calderisi, Jill Moyse, Sandra Palencia, Michael Brown-Palsgrove, Jessica Lovstad, Jillian Braun, Steve Ross, Megan Ross, Audra Meinelt, Josh Hollingsworth, Craig Demitros, Sondra Katzen, Kristen Lukas, Edison Steffenson, and Emily and Wolfgang Fey. We are especially grateful to Maureen Leahy and Sharon Dewar of Lincoln Park Zoo, who generously answered questions, facilitated photography needs, and painstakingly reviewed multiple versions of this manuscript throughout its development. Thanks also to gorilla rock star Eric Meyers and especially to  the multitalented, gracious Jan Parkes for nearly all the adults' baby photos as well as the pictures of Carlos, Hope, Debbie, Frank, Lulu, Mumbah, and Bengati. Jim Davis's unofficial Gorilla Studbook and Tom Parkes's unbelievably encyclopedic memory of U.S. gorillas were essential for our work. Finally, thanks to Laura Godwin, Noa Wheeler, Patrick Collins, Elynn Cohen, Julia Sooy, Lara Stelmaszyk, Kate Hannigan, Michael Singer, and our beloved Marcy Posner for helping to shepherd this book through every stage of the process.

AUTHOR'S NOTE

Azizi looks at pictures with me from five years earlier of Makari (his mom), JoJo (his dad), and Susie (his sister). Azizi's code for wanting to turn a page was to give a little shrug and nod slightly to the right.

For as long as I can remember, I have loved watching and learning about animals. By profession, I am a sociologist, which is a type of social scientist. I study social behavior and how being part of a group influences the ways we behave, including how we think. Mostly I study humans, but I also spend time learning about the social behavior of other animals. Gorillas have found a special place in my heart.

The type of research I do is called ethnography. It involves studying people in the environments where they would normally be found. For instance, we may study families in their homes and workers in their workplaces. Our research is called "fieldwork," just like that of primatologists, who study gorillas living in the wild. Ethnographers talk to the subjects of our study; sometimes we even participate in what they're doing. But our fieldwork also depends on being able to watch people carefully and learn from our observations.

I was teaching at the Illinois Institute of Technology in Chicago when I decided to create a course that would help my students improve their observation skills. Students would watch the gorillas at our local zoo, practicing observing, taking data, and communicating what they saw to others. Most of my students were preparing for careers in design and architecture, so at the end of the course, the students would also propose design concepts to benefit the gorillas. These included objects, services, and habitat features—all based on their observations. (If you are interested in the work students do in this course, see *Watching Closely: A Guide to Ethnographic Observation,* Oxford University Press, 2015.)

Left to right: Sally Limb, Jim Hornor, John Dominski, Eugene Limb, and me at the 2011 Environmental Design Research Association meetings, where we gave a presentation on observation-based research and our work with the gorillas.

It was out of this class that this book was born—my students became my coauthors, and together we developed design principles, created visual elements, and researched this book, using public resources and our eyes and ears in the field. We wanted to share our appreciation of gorillas, both as individuals and as a species. We hope you, too, will find the time to observe gorillas closely—wherever you are on your own journey of discovery with these amazing primates.

—C. N-E.

Miguel Martinez in the photography studio, making radishes and the other gorilla food on pages 136–137 look delicious.

John Dominski ▶ as he is usually seen whenever he is photographing gorillas.

Fred Grier at the London architecture ▶ firm where he works, drawing the world map on pages 22–23.

ABOUT THE
AUTHORS

Christena Nippert-Eng is a sociologist and university professor. She enjoys being with family and friends (of any species), and she likes mysteries, music, and comedy, sometimes all at once.

John Dominski is a design researcher at gravitytank in Chicago. He is an avid photographer and movement enthusiast and has been recently bitten by wanderlust. John is the principal natural photographer for this book.

Frederick Grier is an architect currently working in London, interested in urban environmental design. When he's not designing buildings around the world, Fred enjoys scuba diving, painting, cooking, and cycling.

Jim Hornor is a designer and product manager in Portland, Oregon. When he's not in the office, you'll find him playing fetch with his dog Tildy, gardening, jumping into rivers, reading, eating good food, and laughing.

Eugene Limb is a designer and researcher in the San Francisco Bay Area. He loves creating music, traveling, and experiencing culture through food.

Sally Limb is a user experience designer at Apple in Northern California. She enjoys spending her free time exploring the sights and sounds of San Francisco and planning her next adventure abroad.

Miguel Martinez is an all-around designer and strategist working in Chicago. His many interests include film, photography, games, woodworking, and cats. Miguel is the principle studio and postproduction photographer for this book.

INDEX

Page references in *italics refer to photographs.*